Property Address: _____

House Nickname: _____

NMLS#: _____   Price: ____

#Bedrooms: _____   #Bathrooms: _____   #Car Garage: _____

House sq/ft: _____   Lot sq/ft: _____   Age of House: _____

I0503585

THE HOME

	✗	✓	♥
Exterior Condition	○	○	○
Curve Appeal	○	○	○
Floorplan	○	○	○
Kitchen	○	○	○
Family Room	○	○	○
Dining Room	○	○	○
Laundry Room	○	○	○
Master Bedroom	○	○	○
Master Bathroom	○	○	○
Extra Bedrooms	○	○	○
Extra Bathrooms	○	○	○
Closets	○	○	○
Storage Space	○	○	○
Flooring	○	○	○

THE FEATURES

	✗	✓	♥
Kitchen Cabinets	○	○	○
Kitchen Apppliances	○	○	○
Washer/Dryer	○	○	○
Fireplace	○	○	○
Patio/Balcony	○	○	○
Pool	○	○	○
Landscaping	○	○	○
A/C/Heating	○	○	○
Roof	○	○	○
Windows	○	○	○
Doors	○	○	○
Sprinkler System	○	○	○
Parking	○	○	○
Other	○	○	○

NOTES ABOUT THE NEIGHBORHOOD

Appearance: _____

Traffic: _____

Safety/Security: _____

Schools: _____

HOA: _____

Other: _____

ADDITIONAL NOTES: _____

_____

_____

_____

_____

AGENTS INFORMATION

Agents Name: _____

Agent Phone Number: _____

Open House: _____

OVERALL RATING: ☆ ☆ ☆ ☆ ☆

Property Address: _____
House Nickname: _____
NMLS#: _____ Price: _____
#Bedrooms: _____ #Bathrooms: _____ #Car Garage: _____
House sq/ft: _____ Lot sq/ft: _____ Age of House: _____

THE HOME

	X	✓	♥
Exterior Condition	○	○	○
Curve Appeal	○	○	○
Floorplan	○	○	○
Kitchen	○	○	○
Family Room	○	○	○
Dining Room	○	○	○
Laundry Room	○	○	○
Master Bedroom	○	○	○
Master Bathroom	○	○	○
Extra Bedrooms	○	○	○
Extra Bathrooms	○	○	○
Closets	○	○	○
Storage Space	○	○	○
Flooring	○	○	○

THE FEATURES

	X	✓	♥
Kitchen Cabinets	○	○	○
Kitchen Apppliances	○	○	○
Washer/Dryer	○	○	○
Fireplace	○	○	○
Patio/Balcony	○	○	○
Pool	○	○	○
Landscaping	○	○	○
A/C/Heating	○	○	○
Roof	○	○	○
Windows	○	○	○
Doors	○	○	○
Sprinkler System	○	○	○
Parking	○	○	○
Other	○	○	○

NOTES ABOUT THE NEIGHBORHOOD

Appearance: _____
Traffic: _____
Safety/Security: _____
Schools: _____
HOA: _____
Other: _____

ADDITIONAL NOTES: _____
_____
_____
_____
_____

AGENTS INFORMATION

Agents Name: _____
Agent Phone Number: _____
Open House: _____

OVERALL RATING: ☆ ☆ ☆ ☆ ☆

Property Address: _____

House Nickname: _____

NMLS#: _____ Price: _____

#Bedrooms: _____ #Bathrooms: _____ #Car Garage: _____

House sq/ft: _____ Lot sq/ft: _____ Age of House: _____

THE HOME

	X	✓	♥
Exterior Condition	○	○	○
Curve Appeal	○	○	○
Floorplan	○	○	○
Kitchen	○	○	○
Family Room	○	○	○
Dining Room	○	○	○
Laundry Room	○	○	○
Master Bedroom	○	○	○
Master Bathroom	○	○	○
Extra Bedrooms	○	○	○
Extra Bathrooms	○	○	○
Closets	○	○	○
Storage Space	○	○	○
Flooring	○	○	○

THE FEATURES

	X	✓	♥
Kitchen Cabinets	○	○	○
Kitchen Apppliances	○	○	○
Washer/Dryer	○	○	○
Fireplace	○	○	○
Patio/Balcony	○	○	○
Pool	○	○	○
Landscaping	○	○	○
A/C/Heating	○	○	○
Roof	○	○	○
Windows	○	○	○
Doors	○	○	○
Sprinkler System	○	○	○
Parking	○	○	○
Other	○	○	○

NOTES ABOUT THE NEIGHBORHOOD

Appearance: _____

Traffic: _____

Safety/Security: _____

Schools: _____

HOA: _____

Other: _____

ADDITIONAL NOTES: _____

_____

_____

_____

_____

AGENTS INFORMATION

Agents Name: _____

Agent Phone Number: _____

Open House: _____

OVERALL RATING: ☆☆☆☆☆

Property Address: _____
House Nickname: _____
NMLS#: _____ Price: _____
#Bedrooms: _____ #Bathrooms: _____ #Car Garage: _____
House sq/ft: _____ Lot sq/ft: _____ Age of House: _____

THE HOME

	X	✔	♥
Exterior Condition	○	○	○
Curve Appeal	○	○	○
Floorplan	○	○	○
Kitchen	○	○	○
Family Room	○	○	○
Dining Room	○	○	○
Laundry Room	○	○	○
Master Bedroom	○	○	○
Master Bathroom	○	○	○
Extra Bedrooms	○	○	○
Extra Bathrooms	○	○	○
Closets	○	○	○
Storage Space	○	○	○
Flooring	○	○	○

THE FEATURES

	X	✔	♥
Kitchen Cabinets	○	○	○
Kitchen Apppliances	○	○	○
Washer/Dryer	○	○	○
Fireplace	○	○	○
Patio/Balcony	○	○	○
Pool	○	○	○
Landscaping	○	○	○
A/C/Heating	○	○	○
Roof	○	○	○
Windows	○	○	○
Doors	○	○	○
Sprinkler System	○	○	○
Parking	○	○	○
Other	○	○	○

NOTES ABOUT THE NEIGHBORHOOD

Appearance: _____
Traffic: _____
Safety/Security: _____
Schools: _____
HOA: _____
Other: _____

ADDITIONAL NOTES: _____

_____
_____
_____
_____

AGENTS INFORMATION

Agents Name: _____
Agent Phone Number: _____
Open House: _____

OVERALL RATING: ☆☆☆☆☆

Property Address: _____
House Nickname: _____
NMLS#: _____ Price: _____
#Bedrooms: _____ #Bathrooms: _____ #Car Garage: _____
House sq/ft: _____ Lot sq/ft: _____ Age of House: _____

THE HOME

	X	✔	♥
Exterior Condition	○	○	○
Curve Appeal	○	○	○
Floorplan	○	○	○
Kitchen	○	○	○
Family Room	○	○	○
Dining Room	○	○	○
Laundry Room	○	○	○
Master Bedroom	○	○	○
Master Bathroom	○	○	○
Extra Bedrooms	○	○	○
Extra Bathrooms	○	○	○
Closets	○	○	○
Storage Space	○	○	○
Flooring	○	○	○

THE FEATURES

	X	✔	♥
Kitchen Cabinets	○	○	○
Kitchen Apppliances	○	○	○
Washer/Dryer	○	○	○
Fireplace	○	○	○
Patio/Balcony	○	○	○
Pool	○	○	○
Landscaping	○	○	○
A/C/Heating	○	○	○
Roof	○	○	○
Windows	○	○	○
Doors	○	○	○
Sprinkler System	○	○	○
Parking	○	○	○
Other	○	○	○

NOTES ABOUT THE NEIGHBORHOOD

Appearance: _____
Traffic: _____
Safety/Security: _____
Schools: _____
HOA: _____
Other: _____

ADDITIONAL NOTES: _____
_____
_____
_____
_____

AGENTS INFORMATION

Agents Name: _____
Agent Phone Number: _____
Open House: _____

OVERALL RATING: ☆ ☆ ☆ ☆ ☆

Property Address: _____

House Nickname: _____

NMLS#: _____   Price: _____

#Bedrooms: _____   #Bathrooms: _____   #Car Garage: _____

House sq/ft: _____   Lot sq/ft: _____   Age of House: _____

THE HOME

	✘	✔	♥
Exterior Condition	○	○	○
Curve Appeal	○	○	○
Floorplan	○	○	○
Kitchen	○	○	○
Family Room	○	○	○
Dining Room	○	○	○
Laundry Room	○	○	○
Master Bedroom	○	○	○
Master Bathroom	○	○	○
Extra Bedrooms	○	○	○
Extra Bathrooms	○	○	○
Closets	○	○	○
Storage Space	○	○	○
Flooring	○	○	○

THE FEATURES

	✘	✔	♥
Kitchen Cabinets	○	○	○
Kitchen Apppliances	○	○	○
Washer/Dryer	○	○	○
Fireplace	○	○	○
Patio/Balcony	○	○	○
Pool	○	○	○
Landscaping	○	○	○
A/C/Heating	○	○	○
Roof	○	○	○
Windows	○	○	○
Doors	○	○	○
Sprinkler System	○	○	○
Parking	○	○	○
Other	○	○	○

NOTES ABOUT THE NEIGHBORHOOD

Appearance: _____

Traffic: _____

Safety/Security: _____

Schools: _____

HOA: _____

Other: _____

ADDITIONAL NOTES: _____

_____
_____
_____
_____

AGENTS INFORMATION

Agents Name: _____

Agent Phone Number: _____

Open House: _____

OVERALL RATING: ☆ ☆ ☆ ☆ ☆

Property Address: _____
House Nickname: _____
NMLS#: _____ Price: _____
#Bedrooms: _____ #Bathrooms: _____ #Car Garage: _____
House sq/ft: _____ Lot sq/ft: _____ Age of House: _____

THE HOME

	X	✓	♥
Exterior Condition	○	○	○
Curve Appeal	○	○	○
Floorplan	○	○	○
Kitchen	○	○	○
Family Room	○	○	○
Dining Room	○	○	○
Laundry Room	○	○	○
Master Bedroom	○	○	○
Master Bathroom	○	○	○
Extra Bedrooms	○	○	○
Extra Bathrooms	○	○	○
Closets	○	○	○
Storage Space	○	○	○
Flooring	○	○	○

THE FEATURES

	X	✓	♥
Kitchen Cabinets	○	○	○
Kitchen Apppliances	○	○	○
Washer/Dryer	○	○	○
Fireplace	○	○	○
Patio/Balcony	○	○	○
Pool	○	○	○
Landscaping	○	○	○
A/C/Heating	○	○	○
Roof	○	○	○
Windows	○	○	○
Doors	○	○	○
Sprinkler System	○	○	○
Parking	○	○	○
Other	○	○	○

NOTES ABOUT THE NEIGHBORHOOD

Appearance: _____
Traffic: _____
Safety/Security: _____
Schools: _____
HOA: _____
Other: _____

ADDITIONAL NOTES: _____
_____
_____
_____
_____

AGENTS INFORMATION

Agents Name: _____
Agent Phone Number: _____
Open House: _____

OVERALL RATING: ☆ ☆ ☆ ☆ ☆

Property Address: _____
House Nickname: _____
NMLS#: _____ Price: _____
#Bedrooms: _____ #Bathrooms: _____ #Car Garage: _____
House sq/ft: _____ Lot sq/ft: _____ Age of House: _____

THE HOME

	X	✓	♥
Exterior Condition	○	○	○
Curve Appeal	○	○	○
Floorplan	○	○	○
Kitchen	○	○	○
Family Room	○	○	○
Dining Room	○	○	○
Laundry Room	○	○	○
Master Bedroom	○	○	○
Master Bathroom	○	○	○
Extra Bedrooms	○	○	○
Extra Bathrooms	○	○	○
Closets	○	○	○
Storage Space	○	○	○
Flooring	○	○	○

THE FEATURES

	X	✓	♥
Kitchen Cabinets	○	○	○
Kitchen Apppliances	○	○	○
Washer/Dryer	○	○	○
Fireplace	○	○	○
Patio/Balcony	○	○	○
Pool	○	○	○
Landscaping	○	○	○
A/C/Heating	○	○	○
Roof	○	○	○
Windows	○	○	○
Doors	○	○	○
Sprinkler System	○	○	○
Parking	○	○	○
Other	○	○	○

NOTES ABOUT THE NEIGHBORHOOD

Appearance: _____
Traffic: _____
Safety/Security: _____
Schools: _____
HOA: _____
Other: _____

ADDITIONAL NOTES: _____
_____
_____
_____
_____

AGENTS INFORMATION

Agents Name: _____
Agent Phone Number: _____
Open House: _____

OVERALL RATING: ☆ ☆ ☆ ☆ ☆

Property Address: _____

House Nickname: _____

NMLS#: _____   Price: _____

#Bedrooms: _____   #Bathrooms: _____   #Car Garage: _____

House sq/ft: _____   Lot sq/ft: _____   Age of House: _____

THE HOME

	✗	✓	♥
Exterior Condition	○	○	○
Curve Appeal	○	○	○
Floorplan	○	○	○
Kitchen	○	○	○
Family Room	○	○	○
Dining Room	○	○	○
Laundry Room	○	○	○
Master Bedroom	○	○	○
Master Bathroom	○	○	○
Extra Bedrooms	○	○	○
Extra Bathrooms	○	○	○
Closets	○	○	○
Storage Space	○	○	○
Flooring	○	○	○

THE FEATURES

	✗	✓	♥
Kitchen Cabinets	○	○	○
Kitchen Apppliances	○	○	○
Washer/Dryer	○	○	○
Fireplace	○	○	○
Patio/Balcony	○	○	○
Pool	○	○	○
Landscaping	○	○	○
A/C/Heating	○	○	○
Roof	○	○	○
Windows	○	○	○
Doors	○	○	○
Sprinkler System	○	○	○
Parking	○	○	○
Other	○	○	○

NOTES ABOUT THE NEIGHBORHOOD

Appearance: _____

Traffic: _____

Safety/Security: _____

Schools: _____

HOA: _____

Other: _____

ADDITIONAL NOTES: _____

_____
_____
_____
_____

AGENTS INFORMATION

Agents Name: _____

Agent Phone Number: _____

Open House: _____

OVERALL RATING: ☆ ☆ ☆ ☆ ☆

Property Address: _____

House Nickname: _____

NMLS#: _____ Price: _____

#Bedrooms: _____ #Bathrooms: _____ #Car Garage: _____

House sq/ft: _____ Lot sq/ft: _____ Age of House: _____

THE HOME

	✗	✓	♥
Exterior Condition	○	○	○
Curve Appeal	○	○	○
Floorplan	○	○	○
Kitchen	○	○	○
Family Room	○	○	○
Dining Room	○	○	○
Laundry Room	○	○	○
Master Bedroom	○	○	○
Master Bathroom	○	○	○
Extra Bedrooms	○	○	○
Extra Bathrooms	○	○	○
Closets	○	○	○
Storage Space	○	○	○
Flooring	○	○	○

THE FEATURES

	✗	✓	♥
Kitchen Cabinets	○	○	○
Kitchen Apppliances	○	○	○
Washer/Dryer	○	○	○
Fireplace	○	○	○
Patio/Balcony	○	○	○
Pool	○	○	○
Landscaping	○	○	○
A/C/Heating	○	○	○
Roof	○	○	○
Windows	○	○	○
Doors	○	○	○
Sprinkler System	○	○	○
Parking	○	○	○
Other	○	○	○

NOTES ABOUT THE NEIGHBORHOOD

Appearance: _____

Traffic: _____

Safety/Security: _____

Schools: _____

HOA: _____

Other: _____

ADDITIONAL NOTES: _____

_____

_____

_____

_____

AGENTS INFORMATION

Agents Name: _____

Agent Phone Number: _____

Open House: _____

OVERALL RATING: ☆ ☆ ☆ ☆ ☆

Property Address: _____
House Nickname: _____
NMLS#: _____ Price: _____
#Bedrooms: _____ #Bathrooms: _____ #Car Garage: _____
House sq/ft: _____ Lot sq/ft: _____ Age of House: _____

THE HOME

	X	✔	♥
Exterior Condition	○	○	○
Curve Appeal	○	○	○
Floorplan	○	○	○
Kitchen	○	○	○
Family Room	○	○	○
Dining Room	○	○	○
Laundry Room	○	○	○
Master Bedroom	○	○	○
Master Bathroom	○	○	○
Extra Bedrooms	○	○	○
Extra Bathrooms	○	○	○
Closets	○	○	○
Storage Space	○	○	○
Flooring	○	○	○

THE FEATURES

	X	✔	♥
Kitchen Cabinets	○	○	○
Kitchen Apppliances	○	○	○
Washer/Dryer	○	○	○
Fireplace	○	○	○
Patio/Balcony	○	○	○
Pool	○	○	○
Landscaping	○	○	○
A/C/Heating	○	○	○
Roof	○	○	○
Windows	○	○	○
Doors	○	○	○
Sprinkler System	○	○	○
Parking	○	○	○
Other	○	○	○

NOTES ABOUT THE NEIGHBORHOOD

Appearance: _____
Traffic: _____
Safety/Security: _____
Schools: _____
HOA: _____
Other: _____

ADDITIONAL NOTES: _____
_____
_____
_____
_____

AGENTS INFORMATION

Agents Name: _____
Agent Phone Number: _____
Open House: _____

OVERALL RATING: ☆ ☆ ☆ ☆ ☆

Property Address: _____

House Nickname: _____

NMLS#: _____ Price: _____

#Bedrooms: _____ #Bathrooms: _____ #Car Garage: _____

House sq/ft: _____ Lot sq/ft: _____ Age of House: _____

THE HOME

	X	✓	♥
Exterior Condition	O	O	O
Curve Appeal	O	O	O
Floorplan	O	O	O
Kitchen	O	O	O
Family Room	O	O	O
Dining Room	O	O	O
Laundry Room	O	O	O
Master Bedroom	O	O	O
Master Bathroom	O	O	O
Extra Bedrooms	O	O	O
Extra Bathrooms	O	O	O
Closets	O	O	O
Storage Space	O	O	O
Flooring	O	O	O

THE FEATURES

	X	✓	♥
Kitchen Cabinets	O	O	O
Kitchen Apppliances	O	O	O
Washer/Dryer	O	O	O
Fireplace	O	O	O
Patio/Balcony	O	O	O
Pool	O	O	O
Landscaping	O	O	O
A/C/Heating	O	O	O
Roof	O	O	O
Windows	O	O	O
Doors	O	O	O
Sprinkler System	O	O	O
Parking	O	O	O
Other	O	O	O

NOTES ABOUT THE NEIGHBORHOOD

Appearance: _____

Traffic: _____

Safety/Security: _____

Schools: _____

HOA: _____

Other: _____

ADDITIONAL NOTES: _____

_____

_____

_____

_____

AGENTS INFORMATION

Agents Name: _____

Agent Phone Number: _____

Open House: _____

OVERALL RATING: ☆ ☆ ☆ ☆ ☆

Property Address: _____
House Nickname: _____
NMLS#: _____ Price: _____
#Bedrooms: _____ #Bathrooms: _____ #Car Garage: _____
House sq/ft: _____ Lot sq/ft: _____ Age of House: _____

THE HOME

	X	✓	♥
Exterior Condition	○	○	○
Curve Appeal	○	○	○
Floorplan	○	○	○
Kitchen	○	○	○
Family Room	○	○	○
Dining Room	○	○	○
Laundry Room	○	○	○
Master Bedroom	○	○	○
Master Bathroom	○	○	○
Extra Bedrooms	○	○	○
Extra Bathrooms	○	○	○
Closets	○	○	○
Storage Space	○	○	○
Flooring	○	○	○

THE FEATURES

	X	✓	♥
Kitchen Cabinets	○	○	○
Kitchen Apppliances	○	○	○
Washer/Dryer	○	○	○
Fireplace	○	○	○
Patio/Balcony	○	○	○
Pool	○	○	○
Landscaping	○	○	○
A/C/Heating	○	○	○
Roof	○	○	○
Windows	○	○	○
Doors	○	○	○
Sprinkler System	○	○	○
Parking	○	○	○
Other	○	○	○

NOTES ABOUT THE NEIGHBORHOOD

Appearance: _____
Traffic: _____
Safety/Security: _____
Schools: _____
HOA: _____
Other: _____

ADDITIONAL NOTES: _____
_____
_____
_____
_____

AGENTS INFORMATION

Agents Name: _____
Agent Phone Number: _____
Open House: _____

OVERALL RATING: ☆☆☆☆☆

Property Address: _____

House Nickname: _____

NMLS#: _____   Price: _____

#Bedrooms: _____   #Bathrooms: _____   #Car Garage: _____

House sq/ft: _____   Lot sq/ft: _____   Age of House: _____

THE HOME

	X	✓	♥
Exterior Condition	○	○	○
Curve Appeal	○	○	○
Floorplan	○	○	○
Kitchen	○	○	○
Family Room	○	○	○
Dining Room	○	○	○
Laundry Room	○	○	○
Master Bedroom	○	○	○
Master Bathroom	○	○	○
Extra Bedrooms	○	○	○
Extra Bathrooms	○	○	○
Closets	○	○	○
Storage Space	○	○	○
Flooring	○	○	○

THE FEATURES

	X	✓	♥
Kitchen Cabinets	○	○	○
Kitchen Apppliances	○	○	○
Washer/Dryer	○	○	○
Fireplace	○	○	○
Patio/Balcony	○	○	○
Pool	○	○	○
Landscaping	○	○	○
A/C/Heating	○	○	○
Roof	○	○	○
Windows	○	○	○
Doors	○	○	○
Sprinkler System	○	○	○
Parking	○	○	○
Other	○	○	○

NOTES ABOUT THE NEIGHBORHOOD

Appearance: _____

Traffic: _____

Safety/Security: _____

Schools: _____

HOA: _____

Other: _____

ADDITIONAL NOTES: _____

_____

_____

_____

_____

AGENTS INFORMATION

Agents Name: _____

Agent Phone Number: _____

Open House: _____

OVERALL RATING: ☆ ☆ ☆ ☆ ☆

Property Address: _____
House Nickname: _____
NMLS#: _____ Price: _____
#Bedrooms: _____ #Bathrooms: _____ #Car Garage: _____
House sq/ft: _____ Lot sq/ft: _____ Age of House: _____

THE HOME

	X	✓	♥
Exterior Condition	○	○	○
Curve Appeal	○	○	○
Floorplan	○	○	○
Kitchen	○	○	○
Family Room	○	○	○
Dining Room	○	○	○
Laundry Room	○	○	○
Master Bedroom	○	○	○
Master Bathroom	○	○	○
Extra Bedrooms	○	○	○
Extra Bathrooms	○	○	○
Closets	○	○	○
Storage Space	○	○	○
Flooring	○	○	○

THE FEATURES

	X	✓	♥
Kitchen Cabinets	○	○	○
Kitchen Apppliances	○	○	○
Washer/Dryer	○	○	○
Fireplace	○	○	○
Patio/Balcony	○	○	○
Pool	○	○	○
Landscaping	○	○	○
A/C/Heating	○	○	○
Roof	○	○	○
Windows	○	○	○
Doors	○	○	○
Sprinkler System	○	○	○
Parking	○	○	○
Other	○	○	○

NOTES ABOUT THE NEIGHBORHOOD

Appearance: _____
Traffic: _____
Safety/Security: _____
Schools: _____
HOA: _____
Other: _____

ADDITIONAL NOTES: _____
_____
_____
_____
_____

AGENTS INFORMATION

Agents Name: _____
Agent Phone Number: _____
Open House: _____

OVERALL RATING: ☆☆☆☆☆

Property Address: _____
House Nickname: _____
NMLS#: _____ **Price:** _____
#Bedrooms: _____ **#Bathrooms:** _____ **#Car Garage:** _____
House sq/ft: _____ **Lot sq/ft:** _____ **Age of House:** _____

THE HOME

	X	✔	♥
Exterior Condition	○	○	○
Curve Appeal	○	○	○
Floorplan	○	○	○
Kitchen	○	○	○
Family Room	○	○	○
Dining Room	○	○	○
Laundry Room	○	○	○
Master Bedroom	○	○	○
Master Bathroom	○	○	○
Extra Bedrooms	○	○	○
Extra Bathrooms	○	○	○
Closets	○	○	○
Storage Space	○	○	○
Flooring	○	○	○

THE FEATURES

	X	✔	♥
Kitchen Cabinets	○	○	○
Kitchen Apppliances	○	○	○
Washer/Dryer	○	○	○
Fireplace	○	○	○
Patio/Balcony	○	○	○
Pool	○	○	○
Landscaping	○	○	○
A/C/Heating	○	○	○
Roof	○	○	○
Windows	○	○	○
Doors	○	○	○
Sprinkler System	○	○	○
Parking	○	○	○
Other	○	○	○

NOTES ABOUT THE NEIGHBORHOOD

Appearance: _____
Traffic: _____
Safety/Security: _____
Schools: _____
HOA: _____
Other: _____

ADDITIONAL NOTES: _____
_____
_____
_____
_____

AGENTS INFORMATION

Agents Name: _____
Agent Phone Number: _____
Open House: _____

OVERALL RATING: ☆ ☆ ☆ ☆ ☆

Property Address: _____
House Nickname: _____
NMLS#: _____   Price: _____
#Bedrooms: _____   #Bathrooms: _____   #Car Garage: _____
House sq/ft: _____   Lot sq/ft: _____   Age of House: _____

THE HOME

	X	✓	♥
Exterior Condition	○	○	○
Curve Appeal	○	○	○
Floorplan	○	○	○
Kitchen	○	○	○
Family Room	○	○	○
Dining Room	○	○	○
Laundry Room	○	○	○
Master Bedroom	○	○	○
Master Bathroom	○	○	○
Extra Bedrooms	○	○	○
Extra Bathrooms	○	○	○
Closets	○	○	○
Storage Space	○	○	○
Flooring	○	○	○

THE FEATURES

	X	✓	♥
Kitchen Cabinets	○	○	○
Kitchen Apppliances	○	○	○
Washer/Dryer	○	○	○
Fireplace	○	○	○
Patio/Balcony	○	○	○
Pool	○	○	○
Landscaping	○	○	○
A/C/Heating	○	○	○
Roof	○	○	○
Windows	○	○	○
Doors	○	○	○
Sprinkler System	○	○	○
Parking	○	○	○
Other	○	○	○

NOTES ABOUT THE NEIGHBORHOOD

Appearance: _____
Traffic: _____
Safety/Security: _____
Schools: _____
HOA: _____
Other: _____

ADDITIONAL NOTES: _____
_____
_____
_____
_____

AGENTS INFORMATION

Agents Name: _____
Agent Phone Number: _____
Open House: _____

OVERALL RATING: ☆ ☆ ☆ ☆ ☆

Property Address: _____

House Nickname: _____

NMLS#: _____ Price: _____

#Bedrooms: _____ #Bathrooms: _____ #Car Garage: _____

House sq/ft: _____ Lot sq/ft: _____ Age of House: _____

THE HOME

	✗	✓	♥
Exterior Condition	○	○	○
Curve Appeal	○	○	○
Floorplan	○	○	○
Kitchen	○	○	○
Family Room	○	○	○
Dining Room	○	○	○
Laundry Room	○	○	○
Master Bedroom	○	○	○
Master Bathroom	○	○	○
Extra Bedrooms	○	○	○
Extra Bathrooms	○	○	○
Closets	○	○	○
Storage Space	○	○	○
Flooring	○	○	○

THE FEATURES

	✗	✓	♥
Kitchen Cabinets	○	○	○
Kitchen Apppliances	○	○	○
Washer/Dryer	○	○	○
Fireplace	○	○	○
Patio/Balcony	○	○	○
Pool	○	○	○
Landscaping	○	○	○
A/C/Heating	○	○	○
Roof	○	○	○
Windows	○	○	○
Doors	○	○	○
Sprinkler System	○	○	○
Parking	○	○	○
Other	○	○	○

NOTES ABOUT THE NEIGHBORHOOD

Appearance: _____

Traffic: _____

Safety/Security: _____

Schools: _____

HOA: _____

Other: _____

ADDITIONAL NOTES: _____

_____

_____

_____

_____

AGENTS INFORMATION

Agents Name: _____

Agent Phone Number: _____

Open House: _____

OVERALL RATING: ☆ ☆ ☆ ☆ ☆

Property Address: _____
House Nickname: _____
NMLS#: _____ Price: _____
#Bedrooms: _____ #Bathrooms: _____ #Car Garage: _____
House sq/ft: _____ Lot sq/ft: _____ Age of House: _____

THE HOME

	X	✓	♥
Exterior Condition	○	○	○
Curve Appeal	○	○	○
Floorplan	○	○	○
Kitchen	○	○	○
Family Room	○	○	○
Dining Room	○	○	○
Laundry Room	○	○	○
Master Bedroom	○	○	○
Master Bathroom	○	○	○
Extra Bedrooms	○	○	○
Extra Bathrooms	○	○	○
Closets	○	○	○
Storage Space	○	○	○
Flooring	○	○	○

THE FEATURES

	X	✓	♥
Kitchen Cabinets	○	○	○
Kitchen Apppliances	○	○	○
Washer/Dryer	○	○	○
Fireplace	○	○	○
Patio/Balcony	○	○	○
Pool	○	○	○
Landscaping	○	○	○
A/C/Heating	○	○	○
Roof	○	○	○
Windows	○	○	○
Doors	○	○	○
Sprinkler System	○	○	○
Parking	○	○	○
Other	○	○	○

NOTES ABOUT THE NEIGHBORHOOD

Appearance: _____
Traffic: _____
Safety/Security: _____
Schools: _____
HOA: _____
Other: _____

ADDITIONAL NOTES: _____
_____
_____
_____
_____

AGENTS INFORMATION

Agents Name: _____
Agent Phone Number: _____
Open House: _____

OVERALL RATING: ☆ ☆ ☆ ☆ ☆

Property Address:		

Property Address: _____
House Nickname: _____
NMLS#: _____ Price: _____
#Bedrooms: _____ #Bathrooms: _____ #Car Garage: _____
House sq/ft: _____ Lot sq/ft: _____ Age of House: _____

THE HOME

	X	✓	♥
Exterior Condition	○	○	○
Curve Appeal	○	○	○
Floorplan	○	○	○
Kitchen	○	○	○
Family Room	○	○	○
Dining Room	○	○	○
Laundry Room	○	○	○
Master Bedroom	○	○	○
Master Bathroom	○	○	○
Extra Bedrooms	○	○	○
Extra Bathrooms	○	○	○
Closets	○	○	○
Storage Space	○	○	○
Flooring	○	○	○

THE FEATURES

	X	✓	♥
Kitchen Cabinets	○	○	○
Kitchen Apppliances	○	○	○
Washer/Dryer	○	○	○
Fireplace	○	○	○
Patio/Balcony	○	○	○
Pool	○	○	○
Landscaping	○	○	○
A/C/Heating	○	○	○
Roof	○	○	○
Windows	○	○	○
Doors	○	○	○
Sprinkler System	○	○	○
Parking	○	○	○
Other	○	○	○

NOTES ABOUT THE NEIGHBORHOOD

Appearance: _____
Traffic: _____
Safety/Security: _____
Schools: _____
HOA: _____
Other: _____

ADDITIONAL NOTES: _____
_____
_____
_____
_____

AGENTS INFORMATION

Agents Name: _____
Agent Phone Number: _____
Open House: _____

OVERALL RATING: ☆☆☆☆☆

Property Address: _____
House Nickname: _____
NMLS#: _____ Price: _____
#Bedrooms: _____ #Bathrooms: _____ #Car Garage: _____
House sq/ft: _____ Lot sq/ft: _____ Age of House: _____

THE HOME

	✗	✓	♥
Exterior Condition	○	○	○
Curve Appeal	○	○	○
Floorplan	○	○	○
Kitchen	○	○	○
Family Room	○	○	○
Dining Room	○	○	○
Laundry Room	○	○	○
Master Bedroom	○	○	○
Master Bathroom	○	○	○
Extra Bedrooms	○	○	○
Extra Bathrooms	○	○	○
Closets	○	○	○
Storage Space	○	○	○
Flooring	○	○	○

THE FEATURES

	✗	✓	♥
Kitchen Cabinets	○	○	○
Kitchen Apppliances	○	○	○
Washer/Dryer	○	○	○
Fireplace	○	○	○
Patio/Balcony	○	○	○
Pool	○	○	○
Landscaping	○	○	○
A/C/Heating	○	○	○
Roof	○	○	○
Windows	○	○	○
Doors	○	○	○
Sprinkler System	○	○	○
Parking	○	○	○
Other	○	○	○

NOTES ABOUT THE NEIGHBORHOOD

Appearance: _____
Traffic: _____
Safety/Security: _____
Schools: _____
HOA: _____
Other: _____

ADDITIONAL NOTES: _____
_____
_____
_____
_____

AGENTS INFORMATION

Agents Name: _____
Agent Phone Number: _____
Open House: _____

OVERALL RATING: ☆ ☆ ☆ ☆ ☆

Property Address: _____

House Nickname: _____

NMLS#: _____ Price: _____

#Bedrooms: _____ #Bathrooms: _____ #Car Garage: _____

House sq/ft: _____ Lot sq/ft: _____ Age of House: _____

THE HOME

	X	**✔**	**♥**
Exterior Condition	○	○	○
Curve Appeal	○	○	○
Floorplan	○	○	○
Kitchen	○	○	○
Family Room	○	○	○
Dining Room	○	○	○
Laundry Room	○	○	○
Master Bedroom	○	○	○
Master Bathroom	○	○	○
Extra Bedrooms	○	○	○
Extra Bathrooms	○	○	○
Closets	○	○	○
Storage Space	○	○	○
Flooring	○	○	○

THE FEATURES

	X	**✔**	**♥**
Kitchen Cabinets	○	○	○
Kitchen Apppliances	○	○	○
Washer/Dryer	○	○	○
Fireplace	○	○	○
Patio/Balcony	○	○	○
Pool	○	○	○
Landscaping	○	○	○
A/C/Heating	○	○	○
Roof	○	○	○
Windows	○	○	○
Doors	○	○	○
Sprinkler System	○	○	○
Parking	○	○	○
Other	○	○	○

NOTES ABOUT THE NEIGHBORHOOD

Appearance: _____

Traffic: _____

Safety/Security: _____

Schools: _____

HOA: _____

Other: _____

ADDITIONAL NOTES: _____

_____

_____

_____

_____

AGENTS INFORMATION

Agents Name: _____

Agent Phone Number: _____

Open House: _____

OVERALL RATING: ☆ ☆ ☆ ☆ ☆

Property Address: _____
House Nickname: _____
NMLS#: _____ Price: _____
#Bedrooms: _____ #Bathrooms: _____ #Car Garage: _____
House sq/ft: _____ Lot sq/ft: _____ Age of House: _____

THE HOME

	X	✓	♥
Exterior Condition	○	○	○
Curve Appeal	○	○	○
Floorplan	○	○	○
Kitchen	○	○	○
Family Room	○	○	○
Dining Room	○	○	○
Laundry Room	○	○	○
Master Bedroom	○	○	○
Master Bathroom	○	○	○
Extra Bedrooms	○	○	○
Extra Bathrooms	○	○	○
Closets	○	○	○
Storage Space	○	○	○
Flooring	○	○	○

THE FEATURES

	X	✓	♥
Kitchen Cabinets	○	○	○
Kitchen Apppliances	○	○	○
Washer/Dryer	○	○	○
Fireplace	○	○	○
Patio/Balcony	○	○	○
Pool	○	○	○
Landscaping	○	○	○
A/C/Heating	○	○	○
Roof	○	○	○
Windows	○	○	○
Doors	○	○	○
Sprinkler System	○	○	○
Parking	○	○	○
Other	○	○	○

NOTES ABOUT THE NEIGHBORHOOD

Appearance: _____
Traffic: _____
Safety/Security: _____
Schools: _____
HOA: _____
Other: _____

ADDITIONAL NOTES: _____
_____
_____
_____
_____

AGENTS INFORMATION

Agents Name: _____
Agent Phone Number: _____
Open House: _____

OVERALL RATING: ☆☆☆☆☆

Property Address: _____

House Nickname: _____

NMLS#: _____ Price: _____

#Bedrooms: _____ #Bathrooms: _____ #Car Garage: _____

House sq/ft: _____ Lot sq/ft: _____ Age of House: _____

THE HOME

	X	✓	♥
Exterior Condition	○	○	○
Curve Appeal	○	○	○
Floorplan	○	○	○
Kitchen	○	○	○
Family Room	○	○	○
Dining Room	○	○	○
Laundry Room	○	○	○
Master Bedroom	○	○	○
Master Bathroom	○	○	○
Extra Bedrooms	○	○	○
Extra Bathrooms	○	○	○
Closets	○	○	○
Storage Space	○	○	○
Flooring	○	○	○

THE FEATURES

	X	✓	♥
Kitchen Cabinets	○	○	○
Kitchen Apppliances	○	○	○
Washer/Dryer	○	○	○
Fireplace	○	○	○
Patio/Balcony	○	○	○
Pool	○	○	○
Landscaping	○	○	○
A/C/Heating	○	○	○
Roof	○	○	○
Windows	○	○	○
Doors	○	○	○
Sprinkler System	○	○	○
Parking	○	○	○
Other	○	○	○

NOTES ABOUT THE NEIGHBORHOOD

Appearance: _____

Traffic: _____

Safety/Security: _____

Schools: _____

HOA: _____

Other: _____

ADDITIONAL NOTES: _____

_____

_____

_____

_____

AGENTS INFORMATION

Agents Name: _____

Agent Phone Number: _____

Open House: _____

OVERALL RATING: ☆☆☆☆☆

Property Address: _____
House Nickname: _____
NMLS#: _____ Price: _____
#Bedrooms: _____ #Bathrooms: _____ #Car Garage: _____
House sq/ft: _____ Lot sq/ft: _____ Age of House: _____

THE HOME

	X	✓	♥
Exterior Condition	○	○	○
Curve Appeal	○	○	○
Floorplan	○	○	○
Kitchen	○	○	○
Family Room	○	○	○
Dining Room	○	○	○
Laundry Room	○	○	○
Master Bedroom	○	○	○
Master Bathroom	○	○	○
Extra Bedrooms	○	○	○
Extra Bathrooms	○	○	○
Closets	○	○	○
Storage Space	○	○	○
Flooring	○	○	○

THE FEATURES

	X	✓	♥
Kitchen Cabinets	○	○	○
Kitchen Apppliances	○	○	○
Washer/Dryer	○	○	○
Fireplace	○	○	○
Patio/Balcony	○	○	○
Pool	○	○	○
Landscaping	○	○	○
A/C/Heating	○	○	○
Roof	○	○	○
Windows	○	○	○
Doors	○	○	○
Sprinkler System	○	○	○
Parking	○	○	○
Other	○	○	○

NOTES ABOUT THE NEIGHBORHOOD

Appearance: _____
Traffic: _____
Safety/Security: _____
Schools: _____
HOA: _____
Other: _____

ADDITIONAL NOTES: _____
_____
_____
_____
_____

AGENTS INFORMATION

Agents Name: _____
Agent Phone Number: _____
Open House: _____

OVERALL RATING: ☆ ☆ ☆ ☆ ☆

Property Address: _____
House Nickname: _____
NMLS#: _____ Price: _____
#Bedrooms: _____ #Bathrooms: _____ #Car Garage: _____
House sq/ft: _____ Lot sq/ft: _____ Age of House: _____

THE HOME

	✗	✓	♥
Exterior Condition	○	○	○
Curve Appeal	○	○	○
Floorplan	○	○	○
Kitchen	○	○	○
Family Room	○	○	○
Dining Room	○	○	○
Laundry Room	○	○	○
Master Bedroom	○	○	○
Master Bathroom	○	○	○
Extra Bedrooms	○	○	○
Extra Bathrooms	○	○	○
Closets	○	○	○
Storage Space	○	○	○
Flooring	○	○	○

THE FEATURES

	✗	✓	♥
Kitchen Cabinets	○	○	○
Kitchen Apppliances	○	○	○
Washer/Dryer	○	○	○
Fireplace	○	○	○
Patio/Balcony	○	○	○
Pool	○	○	○
Landscaping	○	○	○
A/C/Heating	○	○	○
Roof	○	○	○
Windows	○	○	○
Doors	○	○	○
Sprinkler System	○	○	○
Parking	○	○	○
Other	○	○	○

NOTES ABOUT THE NEIGHBORHOOD

Appearance: _____
Traffic: _____
Safety/Security: _____
Schools: _____
HOA: _____
Other: _____

ADDITIONAL NOTES: _____
_____
_____
_____
_____

AGENTS INFORMATION

Agents Name: _____
Agent Phone Number: _____
Open House: _____

OVERALL RATING: ☆ ☆ ☆ ☆ ☆

Property Address: _____

House Nickname: _____

NMLS#: _____ Price: _____

#Bedrooms: _____ #Bathrooms: _____ #Car Garage: _____

House sq/ft: _____ Lot sq/ft: _____ Age of House: _____

THE HOME

	✗	✓	♥
Exterior Condition	○	○	○
Curve Appeal	○	○	○
Floorplan	○	○	○
Kitchen	○	○	○
Family Room	○	○	○
Dining Room	○	○	○
Laundry Room	○	○	○
Master Bedroom	○	○	○
Master Bathroom	○	○	○
Extra Bedrooms	○	○	○
Extra Bathrooms	○	○	○
Closets	○	○	○
Storage Space	○	○	○
Flooring	○	○	○

THE FEATURES

	✗	✓	♥
Kitchen Cabinets	○	○	○
Kitchen Apppliances	○	○	○
Washer/Dryer	○	○	○
Fireplace	○	○	○
Patio/Balcony	○	○	○
Pool	○	○	○
Landscaping	○	○	○
A/C/Heating	○	○	○
Roof	○	○	○
Windows	○	○	○
Doors	○	○	○
Sprinkler System	○	○	○
Parking	○	○	○
Other	○	○	○

NOTES ABOUT THE NEIGHBORHOOD

Appearance: _____

Traffic: _____

Safety/Security: _____

Schools: _____

HOA: _____

Other: _____

ADDITIONAL NOTES: _____

_____

_____

_____

_____

AGENTS INFORMATION

Agents Name: _____

Agent Phone Number: _____

Open House: _____

OVERALL RATING: ☆ ☆ ☆ ☆ ☆

Property Address: _____
House Nickname: _____
NMLS#: _____ Price: _____
#Bedrooms: _____ #Bathrooms: _____ #Car Garage: _____
House sq/ft: _____ Lot sq/ft: _____ Age of House: _____

THE HOME

	X	✓	♥
Exterior Condition	○	○	○
Curve Appeal	○	○	○
Floorplan	○	○	○
Kitchen	○	○	○
Family Room	○	○	○
Dining Room	○	○	○
Laundry Room	○	○	○
Master Bedroom	○	○	○
Master Bathroom	○	○	○
Extra Bedrooms	○	○	○
Extra Bathrooms	○	○	○
Closets	○	○	○
Storage Space	○	○	○
Flooring	○	○	○

THE FEATURES

	X	✓	♥
Kitchen Cabinets	○	○	○
Kitchen Apppliances	○	○	○
Washer/Dryer	○	○	○
Fireplace	○	○	○
Patio/Balcony	○	○	○
Pool	○	○	○
Landscaping	○	○	○
A/C/Heating	○	○	○
Roof	○	○	○
Windows	○	○	○
Doors	○	○	○
Sprinkler System	○	○	○
Parking	○	○	○
Other	○	○	○

NOTES ABOUT THE NEIGHBORHOOD

Appearance: _____
Traffic: _____
Safety/Security: _____
Schools: _____
HOA: _____
Other: _____

ADDITIONAL NOTES: _____
_____
_____
_____
_____

AGENTS INFORMATION

Agents Name: _____
Agent Phone Number: _____
Open House: _____

OVERALL RATING: ☆ ☆ ☆ ☆ ☆

Property Address: _____
House Nickname: _____
NMLS#: _____ Price: _____
#Bedrooms: _____ #Bathrooms: _____ #Car Garage: _____
House sq/ft: _____ Lot sq/ft: _____ Age of House: _____

THE HOME

	X	✓	♥
Exterior Condition	◯	◯	◯
Curve Appeal	◯	◯	◯
Floorplan	◯	◯	◯
Kitchen	◯	◯	◯
Family Room	◯	◯	◯
Dining Room	◯	◯	◯
Laundry Room	◯	◯	◯
Master Bedroom	◯	◯	◯
Master Bathroom	◯	◯	◯
Extra Bedrooms	◯	◯	◯
Extra Bathrooms	◯	◯	◯
Closets	◯	◯	◯
Storage Space	◯	◯	◯
Flooring	◯	◯	◯

THE FEATURES

	X	✓	♥
Kitchen Cabinets	◯	◯	◯
Kitchen Apppliances	◯	◯	◯
Washer/Dryer	◯	◯	◯
Fireplace	◯	◯	◯
Patio/Balcony	◯	◯	◯
Pool	◯	◯	◯
Landscaping	◯	◯	◯
A/C/Heating	◯	◯	◯
Roof	◯	◯	◯
Windows	◯	◯	◯
Doors	◯	◯	◯
Sprinkler System	◯	◯	◯
Parking	◯	◯	◯
Other	◯	◯	◯

NOTES ABOUT THE NEIGHBORHOOD

Appearance: _____
Traffic: _____
Safety/Security: _____
Schools: _____
HOA: _____
Other: _____

ADDITIONAL NOTES: _____

_____
_____
_____
_____

AGENTS INFORMATION

Agents Name: _____
Agent Phone Number: _____
Open House: _____

OVERALL RATING: ☆☆☆☆☆

Property Address: _____

House Nickname: _____

NMLS#: _____ Price: _____

#Bedrooms: _____ #Bathrooms: _____ #Car Garage: _____

House sq/ft: _____ Lot sq/ft: _____ Age of House: _____

THE HOME

	X	✓	♥
Exterior Condition	○	○	○
Curve Appeal	○	○	○
Floorplan	○	○	○
Kitchen	○	○	○
Family Room	○	○	○
Dining Room	○	○	○
Laundry Room	○	○	○
Master Bedroom	○	○	○
Master Bathroom	○	○	○
Extra Bedrooms	○	○	○
Extra Bathrooms	○	○	○
Closets	○	○	○
Storage Space	○	○	○
Flooring	○	○	○

THE FEATURES

	X	✓	♥
Kitchen Cabinets	○	○	○
Kitchen Apppliances	○	○	○
Washer/Dryer	○	○	○
Fireplace	○	○	○
Patio/Balcony	○	○	○
Pool	○	○	○
Landscaping	○	○	○
A/C/Heating	○	○	○
Roof	○	○	○
Windows	○	○	○
Doors	○	○	○
Sprinkler System	○	○	○
Parking	○	○	○
Other	○	○	○

NOTES ABOUT THE NEIGHBORHOOD

Appearance: _____

Traffic: _____

Safety/Security: _____

Schools: _____

HOA: _____

Other: _____

ADDITIONAL NOTES: _____

_____
_____
_____
_____

AGENTS INFORMATION

Agents Name: _____

Agent Phone Number: _____

Open House: _____

OVERALL RATING: ☆ ☆ ☆ ☆ ☆

Property Address: _____
House Nickname: _____
NMLS#: _____   Price: _____
#Bedrooms: _____   #Bathrooms: _____   #Car Garage: _____
House sq/ft: _____   Lot sq/ft: _____   Age of House: _____

THE HOME

	X	✓	♥
Exterior Condition	○	○	○
Curve Appeal	○	○	○
Floorplan	○	○	○
Kitchen	○	○	○
Family Room	○	○	○
Dining Room	○	○	○
Laundry Room	○	○	○
Master Bedroom	○	○	○
Master Bathroom	○	○	○
Extra Bedrooms	○	○	○
Extra Bathrooms	○	○	○
Closets	○	○	○
Storage Space	○	○	○
Flooring	○	○	○

THE FEATURES

	X	✓	♥
Kitchen Cabinets	○	○	○
Kitchen Apppliances	○	○	○
Washer/Dryer	○	○	○
Fireplace	○	○	○
Patio/Balcony	○	○	○
Pool	○	○	○
Landscaping	○	○	○
A/C/Heating	○	○	○
Roof	○	○	○
Windows	○	○	○
Doors	○	○	○
Sprinkler System	○	○	○
Parking	○	○	○
Other	○	○	○

NOTES ABOUT THE NEIGHBORHOOD

Appearance: _____
Traffic: _____
Safety/Security: _____
Schools: _____
HOA: _____
Other: _____

ADDITIONAL NOTES: _____
_____
_____
_____
_____

AGENTS INFORMATION

Agents Name: _____
Agent Phone Number: _____
Open House: _____

OVERALL RATING: ☆ ☆ ☆ ☆ ☆

Property Address: _____

House Nickname: _____

NMLS#: _____ Price: _____

#Bedrooms: _____ #Bathrooms: _____ #Car Garage: _____

House sq/ft: _____ Lot sq/ft: _____ Age of House: _____

THE HOME

	X	✓	♥
Exterior Condition	○	○	○
Curve Appeal	○	○	○
Floorplan	○	○	○
Kitchen	○	○	○
Family Room	○	○	○
Dining Room	○	○	○
Laundry Room	○	○	○
Master Bedroom	○	○	○
Master Bathroom	○	○	○
Extra Bedrooms	○	○	○
Extra Bathrooms	○	○	○
Closets	○	○	○
Storage Space	○	○	○
Flooring	○	○	○

THE FEATURES

	X	✓	♥
Kitchen Cabinets	○	○	○
Kitchen Apppliances	○	○	○
Washer/Dryer	○	○	○
Fireplace	○	○	○
Patio/Balcony	○	○	○
Pool	○	○	○
Landscaping	○	○	○
A/C/Heating	○	○	○
Roof	○	○	○
Windows	○	○	○
Doors	○	○	○
Sprinkler System	○	○	○
Parking	○	○	○
Other	○	○	○

NOTES ABOUT THE NEIGHBORHOOD

Appearance: _____

Traffic: _____

Safety/Security: _____

Schools: _____

HOA: _____

Other: _____

ADDITIONAL NOTES: _____

_____

_____

_____

_____

AGENTS INFORMATION

Agents Name: _____

Agent Phone Number: _____

Open House: _____

OVERALL RATING: ☆☆☆☆☆

Property Address: _____
House Nickname: _____
NMLS#: _____ Price: _____
#Bedrooms: _____ #Bathrooms: _____ #Car Garage: _____
House sq/ft: _____ Lot sq/ft: _____ Age of House: _____

THE HOME

	X	✓	♥
Exterior Condition	○	○	○
Curve Appeal	○	○	○
Floorplan	○	○	○
Kitchen	○	○	○
Family Room	○	○	○
Dining Room	○	○	○
Laundry Room	○	○	○
Master Bedroom	○	○	○
Master Bathroom	○	○	○
Extra Bedrooms	○	○	○
Extra Bathrooms	○	○	○
Closets	○	○	○
Storage Space	○	○	○
Flooring	○	○	○

THE FEATURES

	X	✓	♥
Kitchen Cabinets	○	○	○
Kitchen Apppliances	○	○	○
Washer/Dryer	○	○	○
Fireplace	○	○	○
Patio/Balcony	○	○	○
Pool	○	○	○
Landscaping	○	○	○
A/C/Heating	○	○	○
Roof	○	○	○
Windows	○	○	○
Doors	○	○	○
Sprinkler System	○	○	○
Parking	○	○	○
Other	○	○	○

NOTES ABOUT THE NEIGHBORHOOD

Appearance: _____
Traffic: _____
Safety/Security: _____
Schools: _____
HOA: _____
Other: _____

ADDITIONAL NOTES: _____
_____
_____
_____
_____

AGENTS INFORMATION

Agents Name: _____
Agent Phone Number: _____
Open House: _____

OVERALL RATING: ☆ ☆ ☆ ☆ ☆

Property Address: _____

House Nickname: _____

NMLS#: _____   Price: _____

#Bedrooms: _____   #Bathrooms: _____   #Car Garage: _____

House sq/ft: _____   Lot sq/ft: _____   Age of House: _____

THE HOME

	✗	✓	♥
Exterior Condition	○	○	○
Curve Appeal	○	○	○
Floorplan	○	○	○
Kitchen	○	○	○
Family Room	○	○	○
Dining Room	○	○	○
Laundry Room	○	○	○
Master Bedroom	○	○	○
Master Bathroom	○	○	○
Extra Bedrooms	○	○	○
Extra Bathrooms	○	○	○
Closets	○	○	○
Storage Space	○	○	○
Flooring	○	○	○

THE FEATURES

	✗	✓	♥
Kitchen Cabinets	○	○	○
Kitchen Apppliances	○	○	○
Washer/Dryer	○	○	○
Fireplace	○	○	○
Patio/Balcony	○	○	○
Pool	○	○	○
Landscaping	○	○	○
A/C/Heating	○	○	○
Roof	○	○	○
Windows	○	○	○
Doors	○	○	○
Sprinkler System	○	○	○
Parking	○	○	○
Other	○	○	○

NOTES ABOUT THE NEIGHBORHOOD

Appearance: _____

Traffic: _____

Safety/Security: _____

Schools: _____

HOA: _____

Other: _____

ADDITIONAL NOTES: _____

_____

_____

_____

_____

AGENTS INFORMATION

Agents Name: _____

Agent Phone Number: _____

Open House: _____

OVERALL RATING: ☆ ☆ ☆ ☆ ☆

Property Address: _____
House Nickname: _____
NMLS#: _____ Price: _____
#Bedrooms: _____ #Bathrooms: _____ #Car Garage: _____
House sq/ft: _____ Lot sq/ft: _____ Age of House: _____

THE HOME

	X	✓	♥
Exterior Condition	○	○	○
Curve Appeal	○	○	○
Floorplan	○	○	○
Kitchen	○	○	○
Family Room	○	○	○
Dining Room	○	○	○
Laundry Room	○	○	○
Master Bedroom	○	○	○
Master Bathroom	○	○	○
Extra Bedrooms	○	○	○
Extra Bathrooms	○	○	○
Closets	○	○	○
Storage Space	○	○	○
Flooring	○	○	○

THE FEATURES

	X	✓	♥
Kitchen Cabinets	○	○	○
Kitchen Apppliances	○	○	○
Washer/Dryer	○	○	○
Fireplace	○	○	○
Patio/Balcony	○	○	○
Pool	○	○	○
Landscaping	○	○	○
A/C/Heating	○	○	○
Roof	○	○	○
Windows	○	○	○
Doors	○	○	○
Sprinkler System	○	○	○
Parking	○	○	○
Other	○	○	○

NOTES ABOUT THE NEIGHBORHOOD

Appearance: _____
Traffic: _____
Safety/Security: _____
Schools: _____
HOA: _____
Other: _____

ADDITIONAL NOTES: _____
_____
_____
_____
_____

AGENTS INFORMATION

Agents Name: _____
Agent Phone Number: _____
Open House: _____

OVERALL RATING: ☆☆☆☆☆

Property Address: _____

House Nickname: _____

NMLS#: _____ Price: _____

#Bedrooms: _____ #Bathrooms: _____ #Car Garage: _____

House sq/ft: _____ Lot sq/ft: _____ Age of House: _____

THE HOME

	✗	✓	♥
Exterior Condition	○	○	○
Curve Appeal	○	○	○
Floorplan	○	○	○
Kitchen	○	○	○
Family Room	○	○	○
Dining Room	○	○	○
Laundry Room	○	○	○
Master Bedroom	○	○	○
Master Bathroom	○	○	○
Extra Bedrooms	○	○	○
Extra Bathrooms	○	○	○
Closets	○	○	○
Storage Space	○	○	○
Flooring	○	○	○

THE FEATURES

	✗	✓	♥
Kitchen Cabinets	○	○	○
Kitchen Apppliances	○	○	○
Washer/Dryer	○	○	○
Fireplace	○	○	○
Patio/Balcony	○	○	○
Pool	○	○	○
Landscaping	○	○	○
A/C/Heating	○	○	○
Roof	○	○	○
Windows	○	○	○
Doors	○	○	○
Sprinkler System	○	○	○
Parking	○	○	○
Other	○	○	○

NOTES ABOUT THE NEIGHBORHOOD

Appearance: _____

Traffic: _____

Safety/Security: _____

Schools: _____

HOA: _____

Other: _____

ADDITIONAL NOTES: _____

_____

_____

_____

_____

AGENTS INFORMATION

Agents Name: _____

Agent Phone Number: _____

Open House: _____

OVERALL RATING: ☆ ☆ ☆ ☆ ☆

Property Address: _____
House Nickname: _____
NMLS#: _____ Price: _____
#Bedrooms: _____ #Bathrooms: _____ #Car Garage: _____
House sq/ft: _____ Lot sq/ft: _____ Age of House: _____

THE HOME

	✗	✓	♥
Exterior Condition	○	○	○
Curve Appeal	○	○	○
Floorplan	○	○	○
Kitchen	○	○	○
Family Room	○	○	○
Dining Room	○	○	○
Laundry Room	○	○	○
Master Bedroom	○	○	○
Master Bathroom	○	○	○
Extra Bedrooms	○	○	○
Extra Bathrooms	○	○	○
Closets	○	○	○
Storage Space	○	○	○
Flooring	○	○	○

THE FEATURES

	✗	✓	♥
Kitchen Cabinets	○	○	○
Kitchen Appliances	○	○	○
Washer/Dryer	○	○	○
Fireplace	○	○	○
Patio/Balcony	○	○	○
Pool	○	○	○
Landscaping	○	○	○
A/C/Heating	○	○	○
Roof	○	○	○
Windows	○	○	○
Doors	○	○	○
Sprinkler System	○	○	○
Parking	○	○	○
Other	○	○	○

NOTES ABOUT THE NEIGHBORHOOD

Appearance: _____
Traffic: _____
Safety/Security: _____
Schools: _____
HOA: _____
Other: _____

ADDITIONAL NOTES: _____

_____
_____
_____
_____

AGENTS INFORMATION

Agents Name: _____
Agent Phone Number: _____
Open House: _____

OVERALL RATING: ☆ ☆ ☆ ☆ ☆

Property Address: _____

House Nickname: _____

NMLS#: _____ Price: _____

#Bedrooms: _____ #Bathrooms: _____ #Car Garage: _____

House sq/ft: _____ Lot sq/ft: _____ Age of House: _____

THE HOME

	✗	✔	♥
Exterior Condition	○	○	○
Curve Appeal	○	○	○
Floorplan	○	○	○
Kitchen	○	○	○
Family Room	○	○	○
Dining Room	○	○	○
Laundry Room	○	○	○
Master Bedroom	○	○	○
Master Bathroom	○	○	○
Extra Bedrooms	○	○	○
Extra Bathrooms	○	○	○
Closets	○	○	○
Storage Space	○	○	○
Flooring	○	○	○

THE FEATURES

	✗	✔	♥
Kitchen Cabinets	○	○	○
Kitchen Apppliances	○	○	○
Washer/Dryer	○	○	○
Fireplace	○	○	○
Patio/Balcony	○	○	○
Pool	○	○	○
Landscaping	○	○	○
A/C/Heating	○	○	○
Roof	○	○	○
Windows	○	○	○
Doors	○	○	○
Sprinkler System	○	○	○
Parking	○	○	○
Other	○	○	○

NOTES ABOUT THE NEIGHBORHOOD

Appearance: _____

Traffic: _____

Safety/Security: _____

Schools: _____

HOA: _____

Other: _____

ADDITIONAL NOTES: _____

_____

_____

_____

_____

AGENTS INFORMATION

Agents Name: _____

Agent Phone Number: _____

Open House: _____

OVERALL RATING: ☆ ☆ ☆ ☆ ☆

Property Address: _____
House Nickname: _____
NMLS#: _____ Price: _____
#Bedrooms: _____ #Bathrooms: _____ #Car Garage: _____
House sq/ft: _____ Lot sq/ft: _____ Age of House: _____

THE HOME

	✗	✓	♥
Exterior Condition	○	○	○
Curve Appeal	○	○	○
Floorplan	○	○	○
Kitchen	○	○	○
Family Room	○	○	○
Dining Room	○	○	○
Laundry Room	○	○	○
Master Bedroom	○	○	○
Master Bathroom	○	○	○
Extra Bedrooms	○	○	○
Extra Bathrooms	○	○	○
Closets	○	○	○
Storage Space	○	○	○
Flooring	○	○	○

THE FEATURES

	✗	✓	♥
Kitchen Cabinets	○	○	○
Kitchen Apppliances	○	○	○
Washer/Dryer	○	○	○
Fireplace	○	○	○
Patio/Balcony	○	○	○
Pool	○	○	○
Landscaping	○	○	○
A/C/Heating	○	○	○
Roof	○	○	○
Windows	○	○	○
Doors	○	○	○
Sprinkler System	○	○	○
Parking	○	○	○
Other	○	○	○

NOTES ABOUT THE NEIGHBORHOOD

Appearance: _____
Traffic: _____
Safety/Security: _____
Schools: _____
HOA: _____
Other: _____

ADDITIONAL NOTES: _____
_____
_____
_____
_____

AGENTS INFORMATION

Agents Name: _____
Agent Phone Number: _____
Open House: _____

OVERALL RATING: ☆ ☆ ☆ ☆ ☆

Property Address: _____
House Nickname: _____
NMLS#: _____ Price: _____
#Bedrooms: _____ #Bathrooms: _____ #Car Garage: _____
House sq/ft: _____ Lot sq/ft: _____ Age of House: _____

THE HOME

	X	✓	♥
Exterior Condition	○	○	○
Curve Appeal	○	○	○
Floorplan	○	○	○
Kitchen	○	○	○
Family Room	○	○	○
Dining Room	○	○	○
Laundry Room	○	○	○
Master Bedroom	○	○	○
Master Bathroom	○	○	○
Extra Bedrooms	○	○	○
Extra Bathrooms	○	○	○
Closets	○	○	○
Storage Space	○	○	○
Flooring	○	○	○

THE FEATURES

	X	✓	♥
Kitchen Cabinets	○	○	○
Kitchen Apppliances	○	○	○
Washer/Dryer	○	○	○
Fireplace	○	○	○
Patio/Balcony	○	○	○
Pool	○	○	○
Landscaping	○	○	○
A/C/Heating	○	○	○
Roof	○	○	○
Windows	○	○	○
Doors	○	○	○
Sprinkler System	○	○	○
Parking	○	○	○
Other	○	○	○

NOTES ABOUT THE NEIGHBORHOOD

Appearance: _____
Traffic: _____
Safety/Security: _____
Schools: _____
HOA: _____
Other: _____

ADDITIONAL NOTES: _____
_____
_____
_____
_____

AGENTS INFORMATION

Agents Name: _____
Agent Phone Number: _____
Open House: _____

OVERALL RATING: ☆☆☆☆☆

Property Address: _____

House Nickname: _____

NMLS#: _____   Price: _____

#Bedrooms: _____   #Bathrooms: _____   #Car Garage: _____

House sq/ft: _____   Lot sq/ft: _____   Age of House: _____

THE HOME

	✗	✓	♥
Exterior Condition	○	○	○
Curve Appeal	○	○	○
Floorplan	○	○	○
Kitchen	○	○	○
Family Room	○	○	○
Dining Room	○	○	○
Laundry Room	○	○	○
Master Bedroom	○	○	○
Master Bathroom	○	○	○
Extra Bedrooms	○	○	○
Extra Bathrooms	○	○	○
Closets	○	○	○
Storage Space	○	○	○
Flooring	○	○	○

THE FEATURES

	✗	✓	♥
Kitchen Cabinets	○	○	○
Kitchen Apppliances	○	○	○
Washer/Dryer	○	○	○
Fireplace	○	○	○
Patio/Balcony	○	○	○
Pool	○	○	○
Landscaping	○	○	○
A/C/Heating	○	○	○
Roof	○	○	○
Windows	○	○	○
Doors	○	○	○
Sprinkler System	○	○	○
Parking	○	○	○
Other	○	○	○

NOTES ABOUT THE NEIGHBORHOOD

Appearance: _____

Traffic: _____

Safety/Security: _____

Schools: _____

HOA: _____

Other: _____

ADDITIONAL NOTES: _____

_____

_____

_____

_____

AGENTS INFORMATION

Agents Name: _____

Agent Phone Number: _____

Open House: _____

OVERALL RATING: ☆ ☆ ☆ ☆ ☆

Property Address: _____
House Nickname: _____
NMLS#: _____ Price: _____
#Bedrooms: _____ #Bathrooms: _____ #Car Garage: _____
House sq/ft: _____ Lot sq/ft: _____ Age of House: _____

THE HOME

	X	**✓**	**♥**
Exterior Condition	◯	◯	◯
Curve Appeal	◯	◯	◯
Floorplan	◯	◯	◯
Kitchen	◯	◯	◯
Family Room	◯	◯	◯
Dining Room	◯	◯	◯
Laundry Room	◯	◯	◯
Master Bedroom	◯	◯	◯
Master Bathroom	◯	◯	◯
Extra Bedrooms	◯	◯	◯
Extra Bathrooms	◯	◯	◯
Closets	◯	◯	◯
Storage Space	◯	◯	◯
Flooring	◯	◯	◯

THE FEATURES

	X	**✓**	**♥**
Kitchen Cabinets	◯	◯	◯
Kitchen Apppliances	◯	◯	◯
Washer/Dryer	◯	◯	◯
Fireplace	◯	◯	◯
Patio/Balcony	◯	◯	◯
Pool	◯	◯	◯
Landscaping	◯	◯	◯
A/C/Heating	◯	◯	◯
Roof	◯	◯	◯
Windows	◯	◯	◯
Doors	◯	◯	◯
Sprinkler System	◯	◯	◯
Parking	◯	◯	◯
Other	◯	◯	◯

NOTES ABOUT THE NEIGHBORHOOD

Appearance: _____
Traffic: _____
Safety/Security: _____
Schools: _____
HOA: _____
Other: _____

ADDITIONAL NOTES: _____
_____
_____
_____
_____

AGENTS INFORMATION

Agents Name: _____
Agent Phone Number: _____
Open House: _____

OVERALL RATING: ☆☆☆☆☆

Property Address: _____
House Nickname: _____
NMLS#: _____   Price: _____
#Bedrooms: _____   #Bathrooms: _____   #Car Garage: _____
House sq/ft: _____   Lot sq/ft: _____   Age of House: _____

THE HOME

	✗	✓	♥
Exterior Condition	○	○	○
Curve Appeal	○	○	○
Floorplan	○	○	○
Kitchen	○	○	○
Family Room	○	○	○
Dining Room	○	○	○
Laundry Room	○	○	○
Master Bedroom	○	○	○
Master Bathroom	○	○	○
Extra Bedrooms	○	○	○
Extra Bathrooms	○	○	○
Closets	○	○	○
Storage Space	○	○	○
Flooring	○	○	○

THE FEATURES

	✗	✓	♥
Kitchen Cabinets	○	○	○
Kitchen Apppliances	○	○	○
Washer/Dryer	○	○	○
Fireplace	○	○	○
Patio/Balcony	○	○	○
Pool	○	○	○
Landscaping	○	○	○
A/C/Heating	○	○	○
Roof	○	○	○
Windows	○	○	○
Doors	○	○	○
Sprinkler System	○	○	○
Parking	○	○	○
Other	○	○	○

NOTES ABOUT THE NEIGHBORHOOD

Appearance: _____
Traffic: _____
Safety/Security: _____
Schools: _____
HOA: _____
Other: _____

ADDITIONAL NOTES: _____
_____
_____
_____
_____

AGENTS INFORMATION

Agents Name: _____
Agent Phone Number: _____
Open House: _____

OVERALL RATING: ☆ ☆ ☆ ☆ ☆

Property Address: _____
House Nickname: _____
NMLS#: _____ Price: _____
#Bedrooms: _____ #Bathrooms: _____ #Car Garage: _____
House sq/ft: _____ Lot sq/ft: _____ Age of House: _____

THE HOME

	X	✓	♥
Exterior Condition	○	○	○
Curve Appeal	○	○	○
Floorplan	○	○	○
Kitchen	○	○	○
Family Room	○	○	○
Dining Room	○	○	○
Laundry Room	○	○	○
Master Bedroom	○	○	○
Master Bathroom	○	○	○
Extra Bedrooms	○	○	○
Extra Bathrooms	○	○	○
Closets	○	○	○
Storage Space	○	○	○
Flooring	○	○	○

THE FEATURES

	X	✓	♥
Kitchen Cabinets	○	○	○
Kitchen Apppliances	○	○	○
Washer/Dryer	○	○	○
Fireplace	○	○	○
Patio/Balcony	○	○	○
Pool	○	○	○
Landscaping	○	○	○
A/C/Heating	○	○	○
Roof	○	○	○
Windows	○	○	○
Doors	○	○	○
Sprinkler System	○	○	○
Parking	○	○	○
Other	○	○	○

NOTES ABOUT THE NEIGHBORHOOD

Appearance: _____
Traffic: _____
Safety/Security: _____
Schools: _____
HOA: _____
Other: _____

ADDITIONAL NOTES: _____
_____
_____
_____
_____

AGENTS INFORMATION

Agents Name: _____
Agent Phone Number: _____
Open House: _____

OVERALL RATING: ☆ ☆ ☆ ☆ ☆

Property Address: _____
House Nickname: _____
NMLS#: _____ Price: _____
#Bedrooms: _____ #Bathrooms: _____ #Car Garage: _____
House sq/ft: _____ Lot sq/ft: _____ Age of House: _____

THE HOME

	X	**✓**	**♥**
Exterior Condition	○	○	○
Curve Appeal	○	○	○
Floorplan	○	○	○
Kitchen	○	○	○
Family Room	○	○	○
Dining Room	○	○	○
Laundry Room	○	○	○
Master Bedroom	○	○	○
Master Bathroom	○	○	○
Extra Bedrooms	○	○	○
Extra Bathrooms	○	○	○
Closets	○	○	○
Storage Space	○	○	○
Flooring	○	○	○

THE FEATURES

	X	**✓**	**♥**
Kitchen Cabinets	○	○	○
Kitchen Apppliances	○	○	○
Washer/Dryer	○	○	○
Fireplace	○	○	○
Patio/Balcony	○	○	○
Pool	○	○	○
Landscaping	○	○	○
A/C/Heating	○	○	○
Roof	○	○	○
Windows	○	○	○
Doors	○	○	○
Sprinkler System	○	○	○
Parking	○	○	○
Other	○	○	○

NOTES ABOUT THE NEIGHBORHOOD

Appearance: _____
Traffic: _____
Safety/Security: _____
Schools: _____
HOA: _____
Other: _____

ADDITIONAL NOTES: _____
_____
_____
_____
_____

AGENTS INFORMATION

Agents Name: _____
Agent Phone Number: _____
Open House: _____

OVERALL RATING: ☆ ☆ ☆ ☆ ☆

Property Address: _____

House Nickname: _____

NMLS#: _____ Price: _____

#Bedrooms: _____ #Bathrooms: _____ #Car Garage: _____

House sq/ft: _____ Lot sq/ft: _____ Age of House: _____

THE HOME

	X	✓	♥
Exterior Condition	○	○	○
Curve Appeal	○	○	○
Floorplan	○	○	○
Kitchen	○	○	○
Family Room	○	○	○
Dining Room	○	○	○
Laundry Room	○	○	○
Master Bedroom	○	○	○
Master Bathroom	○	○	○
Extra Bedrooms	○	○	○
Extra Bathrooms	○	○	○
Closets	○	○	○
Storage Space	○	○	○
Flooring	○	○	○

THE FEATURES

	X	✓	♥
Kitchen Cabinets	○	○	○
Kitchen Apppliances	○	○	○
Washer/Dryer	○	○	○
Fireplace	○	○	○
Patio/Balcony	○	○	○
Pool	○	○	○
Landscaping	○	○	○
A/C/Heating	○	○	○
Roof	○	○	○
Windows	○	○	○
Doors	○	○	○
Sprinkler System	○	○	○
Parking	○	○	○
Other	○	○	○

NOTES ABOUT THE NEIGHBORHOOD

Appearance: _____

Traffic: _____

Safety/Security: _____

Schools: _____

HOA: _____

Other: _____

ADDITIONAL NOTES: _____

_____

_____

_____

_____

AGENTS INFORMATION

Agents Name: _____

Agent Phone Number: _____

Open House: _____

OVERALL RATING: ☆ ☆ ☆ ☆ ☆

Property Address: _____

House Nickname: _____

NMLS#: _____   Price: _____

#Bedrooms: _____   #Bathrooms: _____   #Car Garage: _____

House sq/ft: _____   Lot sq/ft: _____   Age of House: _____

THE HOME

	✗	✓	♥
Exterior Condition	○	○	○
Curve Appeal	○	○	○
Floorplan	○	○	○
Kitchen	○	○	○
Family Room	○	○	○
Dining Room	○	○	○
Laundry Room	○	○	○
Master Bedroom	○	○	○
Master Bathroom	○	○	○
Extra Bedrooms	○	○	○
Extra Bathrooms	○	○	○
Closets	○	○	○
Storage Space	○	○	○
Flooring	○	○	○

THE FEATURES

	✗	✓	♥
Kitchen Cabinets	○	○	○
Kitchen Apppliances	○	○	○
Washer/Dryer	○	○	○
Fireplace	○	○	○
Patio/Balcony	○	○	○
Pool	○	○	○
Landscaping	○	○	○
A/C/Heating	○	○	○
Roof	○	○	○
Windows	○	○	○
Doors	○	○	○
Sprinkler System	○	○	○
Parking	○	○	○
Other	○	○	○

NOTES ABOUT THE NEIGHBORHOOD

Appearance: _____

Traffic: _____

Safety/Security: _____

Schools: _____

HOA: _____

Other: _____

ADDITIONAL NOTES: _____

_____

_____

_____

_____

AGENTS INFORMATION

Agents Name: _____

Agent Phone Number: _____

Open House: _____

OVERALL RATING: ☆ ☆ ☆ ☆ ☆

Property Address: _____
House Nickname: _____
NMLS#: _____   Price: _____
#Bedrooms: _____   #Bathrooms: _____   #Car Garage: _____
House sq/ft: _____   Lot sq/ft: _____   Age of House: _____

THE HOME

	✗	✓	♥
Exterior Condition	○	○	○
Curve Appeal	○	○	○
Floorplan	○	○	○
Kitchen	○	○	○
Family Room	○	○	○
Dining Room	○	○	○
Laundry Room	○	○	○
Master Bedroom	○	○	○
Master Bathroom	○	○	○
Extra Bedrooms	○	○	○
Extra Bathrooms	○	○	○
Closets	○	○	○
Storage Space	○	○	○
Flooring	○	○	○

THE FEATURES

	✗	✓	♥
Kitchen Cabinets	○	○	○
Kitchen Apppliances	○	○	○
Washer/Dryer	○	○	○
Fireplace	○	○	○
Patio/Balcony	○	○	○
Pool	○	○	○
Landscaping	○	○	○
A/C/Heating	○	○	○
Roof	○	○	○
Windows	○	○	○
Doors	○	○	○
Sprinkler System	○	○	○
Parking	○	○	○
Other	○	○	○

NOTES ABOUT THE NEIGHBORHOOD

Appearance: _____
Traffic: _____
Safety/Security: _____
Schools: _____
HOA: _____
Other: _____

ADDITIONAL NOTES: _____
_____
_____
_____
_____

AGENTS INFORMATION

Agents Name: _____
Agent Phone Number: _____
Open House: _____

OVERALL RATING: ☆ ☆ ☆ ☆ ☆

Property Address: _____
House Nickname: _____
NMLS#: _____   Price: _____
#Bedrooms: _____   #Bathrooms: _____   #Car Garage: _____
House sq/ft: _____   Lot sq/ft: _____   Age of House: _____

THE HOME

	X	✓	♥
Exterior Condition	○	○	○
Curve Appeal	○	○	○
Floorplan	○	○	○
Kitchen	○	○	○
Family Room	○	○	○
Dining Room	○	○	○
Laundry Room	○	○	○
Master Bedroom	○	○	○
Master Bathroom	○	○	○
Extra Bedrooms	○	○	○
Extra Bathrooms	○	○	○
Closets	○	○	○
Storage Space	○	○	○
Flooring	○	○	○

THE FEATURES

	X	✓	♥
Kitchen Cabinets	○	○	○
Kitchen Appliances	○	○	○
Washer/Dryer	○	○	○
Fireplace	○	○	○
Patio/Balcony	○	○	○
Pool	○	○	○
Landscaping	○	○	○
A/C/Heating	○	○	○
Roof	○	○	○
Windows	○	○	○
Doors	○	○	○
Sprinkler System	○	○	○
Parking	○	○	○
Other	○	○	○

NOTES ABOUT THE NEIGHBORHOOD

Appearance: _____
Traffic: _____
Safety/Security: _____
Schools: _____
HOA: _____
Other: _____

ADDITIONAL NOTES: _____

_____
_____
_____
_____

AGENTS INFORMATION

Agents Name: _____
Agent Phone Number: _____
Open House: _____

OVERALL RATING: ☆ ☆ ☆ ☆ ☆

Property Address: _____

House Nickname: _____

NMLS#: _____   Price: _____

#Bedrooms: _____   #Bathrooms: _____   #Car Garage: _____

House sq/ft: _____   Lot sq/ft: _____   Age of House: _____

THE HOME

	✗	✔	♥
Exterior Condition	○	○	○
Curve Appeal	○	○	○
Floorplan	○	○	○
Kitchen	○	○	○
Family Room	○	○	○
Dining Room	○	○	○
Laundry Room	○	○	○
Master Bedroom	○	○	○
Master Bathroom	○	○	○
Extra Bedrooms	○	○	○
Extra Bathrooms	○	○	○
Closets	○	○	○
Storage Space	○	○	○
Flooring	○	○	○

THE FEATURES

	✗	✔	♥
Kitchen Cabinets	○	○	○
Kitchen Apppliances	○	○	○
Washer/Dryer	○	○	○
Fireplace	○	○	○
Patio/Balcony	○	○	○
Pool	○	○	○
Landscaping	○	○	○
A/C/Heating	○	○	○
Roof	○	○	○
Windows	○	○	○
Doors	○	○	○
Sprinkler System	○	○	○
Parking	○	○	○
Other	○	○	○

NOTES ABOUT THE NEIGHBORHOOD

Appearance: _____

Traffic: _____

Safety/Security: _____

Schools: _____

HOA: _____

Other: _____

ADDITIONAL NOTES: _____

_____

_____

_____

_____

AGENTS INFORMATION

Agents Name: _____

Agent Phone Number: _____

Open House: _____

OVERALL RATING: ☆ ☆ ☆ ☆ ☆

Property Address: _____
House Nickname: _____
NMLS#: _____ Price: _____
#Bedrooms: _____ #Bathrooms: _____ #Car Garage: _____
House sq/ft: _____ Lot sq/ft: _____ Age of House: _____

THE HOME

	X	✓	♥
Exterior Condition	○	○	○
Curve Appeal	○	○	○
Floorplan	○	○	○
Kitchen	○	○	○
Family Room	○	○	○
Dining Room	○	○	○
Laundry Room	○	○	○
Master Bedroom	○	○	○
Master Bathroom	○	○	○
Extra Bedrooms	○	○	○
Extra Bathrooms	○	○	○
Closets	○	○	○
Storage Space	○	○	○
Flooring	○	○	○

THE FEATURES

	X	✓	♥
Kitchen Cabinets	○	○	○
Kitchen Apppliances	○	○	○
Washer/Dryer	○	○	○
Fireplace	○	○	○
Patio/Balcony	○	○	○
Pool	○	○	○
Landscaping	○	○	○
A/C/Heating	○	○	○
Roof	○	○	○
Windows	○	○	○
Doors	○	○	○
Sprinkler System	○	○	○
Parking	○	○	○
Other	○	○	○

NOTES ABOUT THE NEIGHBORHOOD

Appearance: _____
Traffic: _____
Safety/Security: _____
Schools: _____
HOA: _____
Other: _____

ADDITIONAL NOTES: _____
_____
_____
_____
_____

AGENTS INFORMATION

Agents Name: _____
Agent Phone Number: _____
Open House: _____

OVERALL RATING: ☆ ☆ ☆ ☆ ☆

Property Address: _____

House Nickname: _____

NMLS#: _____ Price: _____

#Bedrooms: _____ #Bathrooms: _____ #Car Garage: _____

House sq/ft: _____ Lot sq/ft: _____ Age of House: _____

THE HOME

	X	✓	♥
Exterior Condition	○	○	○
Curve Appeal	○	○	○
Floorplan	○	○	○
Kitchen	○	○	○
Family Room	○	○	○
Dining Room	○	○	○
Laundry Room	○	○	○
Master Bedroom	○	○	○
Master Bathroom	○	○	○
Extra Bedrooms	○	○	○
Extra Bathrooms	○	○	○
Closets	○	○	○
Storage Space	○	○	○
Flooring	○	○	○

THE FEATURES

	X	✓	♥
Kitchen Cabinets	○	○	○
Kitchen Apppliances	○	○	○
Washer/Dryer	○	○	○
Fireplace	○	○	○
Patio/Balcony	○	○	○
Pool	○	○	○
Landscaping	○	○	○
A/C/Heating	○	○	○
Roof	○	○	○
Windows	○	○	○
Doors	○	○	○
Sprinkler System	○	○	○
Parking	○	○	○
Other	○	○	○

NOTES ABOUT THE NEIGHBORHOOD

Appearance: _____

Traffic: _____

Safety/Security: _____

Schools: _____

HOA: _____

Other: _____

ADDITIONAL NOTES: _____

_____

_____

_____

_____

AGENTS INFORMATION

Agents Name: _____

Agent Phone Number: _____

Open House: _____

OVERALL RATING: ☆ ☆ ☆ ☆ ☆

Property Address: _____
House Nickname: _____
NMLS#: _____   Price: _____
#Bedrooms: _____   #Bathrooms: _____   #Car Garage: _____
House sq/ft: _____   Lot sq/ft: _____   Age of House: _____

THE HOME

	✗	✓	♥
Exterior Condition	○	○	○
Curve Appeal	○	○	○
Floorplan	○	○	○
Kitchen	○	○	○
Family Room	○	○	○
Dining Room	○	○	○
Laundry Room	○	○	○
Master Bedroom	○	○	○
Master Bathroom	○	○	○
Extra Bedrooms	○	○	○
Extra Bathrooms	○	○	○
Closets	○	○	○
Storage Space	○	○	○
Flooring	○	○	○

THE FEATURES

	✗	✓	♥
Kitchen Cabinets	○	○	○
Kitchen Apppliances	○	○	○
Washer/Dryer	○	○	○
Fireplace	○	○	○
Patio/Balcony	○	○	○
Pool	○	○	○
Landscaping	○	○	○
A/C/Heating	○	○	○
Roof	○	○	○
Windows	○	○	○
Doors	○	○	○
Sprinkler System	○	○	○
Parking	○	○	○
Other	○	○	○

NOTES ABOUT THE NEIGHBORHOOD

Appearance: _____
Traffic: _____
Safety/Security: _____
Schools: _____
HOA: _____
Other: _____

ADDITIONAL NOTES: _____

_____
_____
_____
_____

AGENTS INFORMATION

Agents Name: _____
Agent Phone Number: _____
Open House: _____

OVERALL RATING: ☆ ☆ ☆ ☆ ☆

Property Address: _____

House Nickname: _____

NMLS#: _____ Price: _____

#Bedrooms: _____ #Bathrooms: _____ #Car Garage: _____

House sq/ft: _____ Lot sq/ft: _____ Age of House: _____

THE HOME

	X	**✓**	**♥**
Exterior Condition	○	○	○
Curve Appeal	○	○	○
Floorplan	○	○	○
Kitchen	○	○	○
Family Room	○	○	○
Dining Room	○	○	○
Laundry Room	○	○	○
Master Bedroom	○	○	○
Master Bathroom	○	○	○
Extra Bedrooms	○	○	○
Extra Bathrooms	○	○	○
Closets	○	○	○
Storage Space	○	○	○
Flooring	○	○	○

THE FEATURES

	X	**✓**	**♥**
Kitchen Cabinets	○	○	○
Kitchen Apppliances	○	○	○
Washer/Dryer	○	○	○
Fireplace	○	○	○
Patio/Balcony	○	○	○
Pool	○	○	○
Landscaping	○	○	○
A/C/Heating	○	○	○
Roof	○	○	○
Windows	○	○	○
Doors	○	○	○
Sprinkler System	○	○	○
Parking	○	○	○
Other	○	○	○

NOTES ABOUT THE NEIGHBORHOOD

Appearance: _____

Traffic: _____

Safety/Security: _____

Schools: _____

HOA: _____

Other: _____

ADDITIONAL NOTES: _____

_____
_____
_____
_____

AGENTS INFORMATION

Agents Name: _____

Agent Phone Number: _____

Open House: _____

OVERALL RATING: ☆☆☆☆☆

Property Address: _____
House Nickname: _____
NMLS#: _____ Price: _____
#Bedrooms: _____ #Bathrooms: _____ #Car Garage: _____
House sq/ft: _____ Lot sq/ft: _____ Age of House: _____

THE HOME

	X	✓	♥
Exterior Condition	○	○	○
Curve Appeal	○	○	○
Floorplan	○	○	○
Kitchen	○	○	○
Family Room	○	○	○
Dining Room	○	○	○
Laundry Room	○	○	○
Master Bedroom	○	○	○
Master Bathroom	○	○	○
Extra Bedrooms	○	○	○
Extra Bathrooms	○	○	○
Closets	○	○	○
Storage Space	○	○	○
Flooring	○	○	○

THE FEATURES

	X	✓	♥
Kitchen Cabinets	○	○	○
Kitchen Apppliances	○	○	○
Washer/Dryer	○	○	○
Fireplace	○	○	○
Patio/Balcony	○	○	○
Pool	○	○	○
Landscaping	○	○	○
A/C/Heating	○	○	○
Roof	○	○	○
Windows	○	○	○
Doors	○	○	○
Sprinkler System	○	○	○
Parking	○	○	○
Other	○	○	○

NOTES ABOUT THE NEIGHBORHOOD

Appearance: _____
Traffic: _____
Safety/Security: _____
Schools: _____
HOA: _____
Other: _____

ADDITIONAL NOTES: _____

_____
_____
_____
_____

AGENTS INFORMATION

Agents Name: _____
Agent Phone Number: _____
Open House: _____

OVERALL RATING: ☆ ☆ ☆ ☆ ☆

Property Address: _____
House Nickname: _____
NMLS#: _____   Price: _____
#Bedrooms: _____   #Bathrooms: _____   #Car Garage: _____
House sq/ft: _____   Lot sq/ft: _____   Age of House: _____

THE HOME

	X	✔	♥
Exterior Condition	○	○	○
Curve Appeal	○	○	○
Floorplan	○	○	○
Kitchen	○	○	○
Family Room	○	○	○
Dining Room	○	○	○
Laundry Room	○	○	○
Master Bedroom	○	○	○
Master Bathroom	○	○	○
Extra Bedrooms	○	○	○
Extra Bathrooms	○	○	○
Closets	○	○	○
Storage Space	○	○	○
Flooring	○	○	○

THE FEATURES

	X	✔	♥
Kitchen Cabinets	○	○	○
Kitchen Apppliances	○	○	○
Washer/Dryer	○	○	○
Fireplace	○	○	○
Patio/Balcony	○	○	○
Pool	○	○	○
Landscaping	○	○	○
A/C/Heating	○	○	○
Roof	○	○	○
Windows	○	○	○
Doors	○	○	○
Sprinkler System	○	○	○
Parking	○	○	○
Other	○	○	○

NOTES ABOUT THE NEIGHBORHOOD

Appearance: _____
Traffic: _____
Safety/Security: _____
Schools: _____
HOA: _____
Other: _____

ADDITIONAL NOTES: _____

_____
_____
_____
_____

AGENTS INFORMATION

Agents Name: _____
Agent Phone Number: _____
Open House: _____

OVERALL RATING: ☆ ☆ ☆ ☆ ☆

Property Address: _____
House Nickname: _____
NMLS#: _____   Price: _____
#Bedrooms: _____   #Bathrooms: _____   #Car Garage: _____
House sq/ft: _____   Lot sq/ft: _____   Age of House: _____

THE HOME

	X	✓	♥
Exterior Condition	○	○	○
Curve Appeal	○	○	○
Floorplan	○	○	○
Kitchen	○	○	○
Family Room	○	○	○
Dining Room	○	○	○
Laundry Room	○	○	○
Master Bedroom	○	○	○
Master Bathroom	○	○	○
Extra Bedrooms	○	○	○
Extra Bathrooms	○	○	○
Closets	○	○	○
Storage Space	○	○	○
Flooring	○	○	○

THE FEATURES

	X	✓	♥
Kitchen Cabinets	○	○	○
Kitchen Apppliances	○	○	○
Washer/Dryer	○	○	○
Fireplace	○	○	○
Patio/Balcony	○	○	○
Pool	○	○	○
Landscaping	○	○	○
A/C/Heating	○	○	○
Roof	○	○	○
Windows	○	○	○
Doors	○	○	○
Sprinkler System	○	○	○
Parking	○	○	○
Other	○	○	○

NOTES ABOUT THE NEIGHBORHOOD

Appearance: _____
Traffic: _____
Safety/Security: _____
Schools: _____
HOA: _____
Other: _____

ADDITIONAL NOTES: _____

_____
_____
_____
_____

AGENTS INFORMATION

Agents Name: _____
Agent Phone Number: _____
Open House: _____

OVERALL RATING: ☆ ☆ ☆ ☆ ☆

Property Address: _____

House Nickname: _____

NMLS#: _____ Price: _____

#Bedrooms: _____ #Bathrooms: _____ #Car Garage: _____

House sq/ft: _____ Lot sq/ft: _____ Age of House: _____

THE HOME

	✗	✓	♥
Exterior Condition	○	○	○
Curve Appeal	○	○	○
Floorplan	○	○	○
Kitchen	○	○	○
Family Room	○	○	○
Dining Room	○	○	○
Laundry Room	○	○	○
Master Bedroom	○	○	○
Master Bathroom	○	○	○
Extra Bedrooms	○	○	○
Extra Bathrooms	○	○	○
Closets	○	○	○
Storage Space	○	○	○
Flooring	○	○	○

THE FEATURES

	✗	✓	♥
Kitchen Cabinets	○	○	○
Kitchen Apppliances	○	○	○
Washer/Dryer	○	○	○
Fireplace	○	○	○
Patio/Balcony	○	○	○
Pool	○	○	○
Landscaping	○	○	○
A/C/Heating	○	○	○
Roof	○	○	○
Windows	○	○	○
Doors	○	○	○
Sprinkler System	○	○	○
Parking	○	○	○
Other	○	○	○

NOTES ABOUT THE NEIGHBORHOOD

Appearance: _____

Traffic: _____

Safety/Security: _____

Schools: _____

HOA: _____

Other: _____

ADDITIONAL NOTES: _____

_____

_____

_____

_____

AGENTS INFORMATION

Agents Name: _____

Agent Phone Number: _____

Open House: _____

OVERALL RATING: ☆ ☆ ☆ ☆ ☆

Property Address: _____

House Nickname: _____

NMLS#: _____ Price: _____

#Bedrooms: _____ #Bathrooms: _____ #Car Garage: _____

House sq/ft: _____ Lot sq/ft: _____ Age of House: _____

THE HOME

	X	✓	♥
Exterior Condition	○	○	○
Curve Appeal	○	○	○
Floorplan	○	○	○
Kitchen	○	○	○
Family Room	○	○	○
Dining Room	○	○	○
Laundry Room	○	○	○
Master Bedroom	○	○	○
Master Bathroom	○	○	○
Extra Bedrooms	○	○	○
Extra Bathrooms	○	○	○
Closets	○	○	○
Storage Space	○	○	○
Flooring	○	○	○

THE FEATURES

	X	✓	♥
Kitchen Cabinets	○	○	○
Kitchen Apppliances	○	○	○
Washer/Dryer	○	○	○
Fireplace	○	○	○
Patio/Balcony	○	○	○
Pool	○	○	○
Landscaping	○	○	○
A/C/Heating	○	○	○
Roof	○	○	○
Windows	○	○	○
Doors	○	○	○
Sprinkler System	○	○	○
Parking	○	○	○
Other	○	○	○

NOTES ABOUT THE NEIGHBORHOOD

Appearance: _____

Traffic: _____

Safety/Security: _____

Schools: _____

HOA: _____

Other: _____

ADDITIONAL NOTES: _____

_____

_____

_____

_____

AGENTS INFORMATION

Agents Name: _____

Agent Phone Number: _____

Open House: _____

OVERALL RATING: ☆☆☆☆☆

Property Address: _____
House Nickname: _____
NMLS#: _____ Price: _____
#Bedrooms: _____ #Bathrooms: _____ #Car Garage: _____
House sq/ft: _____ Lot sq/ft: _____ Age of House: _____

THE HOME

	✗	✓	♥
Exterior Condition	○	○	○
Curve Appeal	○	○	○
Floorplan	○	○	○
Kitchen	○	○	○
Family Room	○	○	○
Dining Room	○	○	○
Laundry Room	○	○	○
Master Bedroom	○	○	○
Master Bathroom	○	○	○
Extra Bedrooms	○	○	○
Extra Bathrooms	○	○	○
Closets	○	○	○
Storage Space	○	○	○
Flooring	○	○	○

THE FEATURES

	✗	✓	♥
Kitchen Cabinets	○	○	○
Kitchen Apppliances	○	○	○
Washer/Dryer	○	○	○
Fireplace	○	○	○
Patio/Balcony	○	○	○
Pool	○	○	○
Landscaping	○	○	○
A/C/Heating	○	○	○
Roof	○	○	○
Windows	○	○	○
Doors	○	○	○
Sprinkler System	○	○	○
Parking	○	○	○
Other	○	○	○

NOTES ABOUT THE NEIGHBORHOOD

Appearance: _____
Traffic: _____
Safety/Security: _____
Schools: _____
HOA: _____
Other: _____

ADDITIONAL NOTES: _____

_____
_____
_____
_____

AGENTS INFORMATION

Agents Name: _____
Agent Phone Number: _____
Open House: _____

OVERALL RATING: ☆ ☆ ☆ ☆ ☆

Property Address: _____
House Nickname: _____
NMLS#: _____ Price: _____
#Bedrooms: _____ #Bathrooms: _____ #Car Garage: _____
House sq/ft: _____ Lot sq/ft: _____ Age of House: _____

THE HOME

	X	✓	♥
Exterior Condition	○	○	○
Curve Appeal	○	○	○
Floorplan	○	○	○
Kitchen	○	○	○
Family Room	○	○	○
Dining Room	○	○	○
Laundry Room	○	○	○
Master Bedroom	○	○	○
Master Bathroom	○	○	○
Extra Bedrooms	○	○	○
Extra Bathrooms	○	○	○
Closets	○	○	○
Storage Space	○	○	○
Flooring	○	○	○

THE FEATURES

	X	✓	♥
Kitchen Cabinets	○	○	○
Kitchen Apppliances	○	○	○
Washer/Dryer	○	○	○
Fireplace	○	○	○
Patio/Balcony	○	○	○
Pool	○	○	○
Landscaping	○	○	○
A/C/Heating	○	○	○
Roof	○	○	○
Windows	○	○	○
Doors	○	○	○
Sprinkler System	○	○	○
Parking	○	○	○
Other	○	○	○

NOTES ABOUT THE NEIGHBORHOOD

Appearance: _____
Traffic: _____
Safety/Security: _____
Schools: _____
HOA: _____
Other: _____

ADDITIONAL NOTES: _____
_____
_____
_____
_____

AGENTS INFORMATION

Agents Name: _____
Agent Phone Number: _____
Open House: _____

OVERALL RATING: ☆ ☆ ☆ ☆ ☆

| Property Address: _____ |
| House Nickname: _____ |
| NMLS#: _____ Price: _____ |
| #Bedrooms: _____ #Bathrooms: _____ #Car Garage: _____ |
| House sq/ft: _____ Lot sq/ft: _____ Age of House: _____ |

THE HOME

	X	✓	♥
Exterior Condition	○	○	○
Curve Appeal	○	○	○
Floorplan	○	○	○
Kitchen	○	○	○
Family Room	○	○	○
Dining Room	○	○	○
Laundry Room	○	○	○
Master Bedroom	○	○	○
Master Bathroom	○	○	○
Extra Bedrooms	○	○	○
Extra Bathrooms	○	○	○
Closets	○	○	○
Storage Space	○	○	○
Flooring	○	○	○

THE FEATURES

	X	✓	♥
Kitchen Cabinets	○	○	○
Kitchen Apppliances	○	○	○
Washer/Dryer	○	○	○
Fireplace	○	○	○
Patio/Balcony	○	○	○
Pool	○	○	○
Landscaping	○	○	○
A/C/Heating	○	○	○
Roof	○	○	○
Windows	○	○	○
Doors	○	○	○
Sprinkler System	○	○	○
Parking	○	○	○
Other	○	○	○

NOTES ABOUT THE NEIGHBORHOOD

Appearance: _____
Traffic: _____
Safety/Security: _____
Schools: _____
HOA: _____
Other: _____

ADDITIONAL NOTES: _____

_____
_____
_____
_____

AGENTS INFORMATION

Agents Name: _____
Agent Phone Number: _____
Open House: _____

OVERALL RATING: ☆☆☆☆☆

Property Address: _____
House Nickname: _____
NMLS#: _____ Price: _____
#Bedrooms: _____ #Bathrooms: _____ #Car Garage: _____
House sq/ft: _____ Lot sq/ft: _____ Age of House: _____

THE HOME

	X	✓	♥
Exterior Condition	○	○	○
Curve Appeal	○	○	○
Floorplan	○	○	○
Kitchen	○	○	○
Family Room	○	○	○
Dining Room	○	○	○
Laundry Room	○	○	○
Master Bedroom	○	○	○
Master Bathroom	○	○	○
Extra Bedrooms	○	○	○
Extra Bathrooms	○	○	○
Closets	○	○	○
Storage Space	○	○	○
Flooring	○	○	○

THE FEATURES

	X	✓	♥
Kitchen Cabinets	○	○	○
Kitchen Apppliances	○	○	○
Washer/Dryer	○	○	○
Fireplace	○	○	○
Patio/Balcony	○	○	○
Pool	○	○	○
Landscaping	○	○	○
A/C/Heating	○	○	○
Roof	○	○	○
Windows	○	○	○
Doors	○	○	○
Sprinkler System	○	○	○
Parking	○	○	○
Other	○	○	○

NOTES ABOUT THE NEIGHBORHOOD

Appearance: _____
Traffic: _____
Safety/Security: _____
Schools: _____
HOA: _____
Other: _____

ADDITIONAL NOTES: _____
_____
_____
_____
_____

AGENTS INFORMATION

Agents Name: _____
Agent Phone Number: _____
Open House: _____

OVERALL RATING: ☆☆☆☆☆

Property Address: _____

House Nickname: _____

NMLS#: _____ Price: _____

#Bedrooms: _____ #Bathrooms: _____ #Car Garage: _____

House sq/ft: _____ Lot sq/ft: _____ Age of House: _____

THE HOME

	X	✓	♥
Exterior Condition	◯	◯	◯
Curve Appeal	◯	◯	◯
Floorplan	◯	◯	◯
Kitchen	◯	◯	◯
Family Room	◯	◯	◯
Dining Room	◯	◯	◯
Laundry Room	◯	◯	◯
Master Bedroom	◯	◯	◯
Master Bathroom	◯	◯	◯
Extra Bedrooms	◯	◯	◯
Extra Bathrooms	◯	◯	◯
Closets	◯	◯	◯
Storage Space	◯	◯	◯
Flooring	◯	◯	◯

THE FEATURES

	X	✓	♥
Kitchen Cabinets	◯	◯	◯
Kitchen Apppliances	◯	◯	◯
Washer/Dryer	◯	◯	◯
Fireplace	◯	◯	◯
Patio/Balcony	◯	◯	◯
Pool	◯	◯	◯
Landscaping	◯	◯	◯
A/C/Heating	◯	◯	◯
Roof	◯	◯	◯
Windows	◯	◯	◯
Doors	◯	◯	◯
Sprinkler System	◯	◯	◯
Parking	◯	◯	◯
Other	◯	◯	◯

NOTES ABOUT THE NEIGHBORHOOD

Appearance: _____

Traffic: _____

Safety/Security: _____

Schools: _____

HOA: _____

Other: _____

ADDITIONAL NOTES: _____

_____

_____

_____

_____

AGENTS INFORMATION

Agents Name: _____

Agent Phone Number: _____

Open House: _____

OVERALL RATING: ☆ ☆ ☆ ☆ ☆

Property Address: _____

House Nickname: _____

NMLS#: _____ Price: _____

#Bedrooms: _____ #Bathrooms: _____ #Car Garage: _____

House sq/ft: _____ Lot sq/ft: _____ Age of House: _____

THE HOME

	X	✓	♥
Exterior Condition	○	○	○
Curve Appeal	○	○	○
Floorplan	○	○	○
Kitchen	○	○	○
Family Room	○	○	○
Dining Room	○	○	○
Laundry Room	○	○	○
Master Bedroom	○	○	○
Master Bathroom	○	○	○
Extra Bedrooms	○	○	○
Extra Bathrooms	○	○	○
Closets	○	○	○
Storage Space	○	○	○
Flooring	○	○	○

THE FEATURES

	X	✓	♥
Kitchen Cabinets	○	○	○
Kitchen Apppliances	○	○	○
Washer/Dryer	○	○	○
Fireplace	○	○	○
Patio/Balcony	○	○	○
Pool	○	○	○
Landscaping	○	○	○
A/C/Heating	○	○	○
Roof	○	○	○
Windows	○	○	○
Doors	○	○	○
Sprinkler System	○	○	○
Parking	○	○	○
Other	○	○	○

NOTES ABOUT THE NEIGHBORHOOD

Appearance: _____

Traffic: _____

Safety/Security: _____

Schools: _____

HOA: _____

Other: _____

ADDITIONAL NOTES: _____

_____

_____

_____

_____

AGENTS INFORMATION

Agents Name: _____

Agent Phone Number: _____

Open House: _____

OVERALL RATING: ☆☆☆☆☆

Property Address: _____

House Nickname: _____

NMLS#: _____ Price: _____

#Bedrooms: _____ #Bathrooms: _____ #Car Garage: _____

House sq/ft: _____ Lot sq/ft: _____ Age of House: _____

THE HOME

	X	✓	♥
Exterior Condition	○	○	○
Curve Appeal	○	○	○
Floorplan	○	○	○
Kitchen	○	○	○
Family Room	○	○	○
Dining Room	○	○	○
Laundry Room	○	○	○
Master Bedroom	○	○	○
Master Bathroom	○	○	○
Extra Bedrooms	○	○	○
Extra Bathrooms	○	○	○
Closets	○	○	○
Storage Space	○	○	○
Flooring	○	○	○

THE FEATURES

	X	✓	♥
Kitchen Cabinets	○	○	○
Kitchen Apppliances	○	○	○
Washer/Dryer	○	○	○
Fireplace	○	○	○
Patio/Balcony	○	○	○
Pool	○	○	○
Landscaping	○	○	○
A/C/Heating	○	○	○
Roof	○	○	○
Windows	○	○	○
Doors	○	○	○
Sprinkler System	○	○	○
Parking	○	○	○
Other	○	○	○

NOTES ABOUT THE NEIGHBORHOOD

Appearance: _____

Traffic: _____

Safety/Security: _____

Schools: _____

HOA: _____

Other: _____

ADDITIONAL NOTES: _____

_____

_____

_____

_____

AGENTS INFORMATION

Agents Name: _____

Agent Phone Number: _____

Open House: _____

OVERALL RATING: ☆ ☆ ☆ ☆ ☆

Property Address: _____
House Nickname: _____
NMLS#: _____ Price: _____
#Bedrooms: _____ #Bathrooms: _____ #Car Garage: _____
House sq/ft: _____ Lot sq/ft: _____ Age of House: _____

THE HOME

	X	✓	♥
Exterior Condition	○	○	○
Curve Appeal	○	○	○
Floorplan	○	○	○
Kitchen	○	○	○
Family Room	○	○	○
Dining Room	○	○	○
Laundry Room	○	○	○
Master Bedroom	○	○	○
Master Bathroom	○	○	○
Extra Bedrooms	○	○	○
Extra Bathrooms	○	○	○
Closets	○	○	○
Storage Space	○	○	○
Flooring	○	○	○

THE FEATURES

	X	✓	♥
Kitchen Cabinets	○	○	○
Kitchen Apppliances	○	○	○
Washer/Dryer	○	○	○
Fireplace	○	○	○
Patio/Balcony	○	○	○
Pool	○	○	○
Landscaping	○	○	○
A/C/Heating	○	○	○
Roof	○	○	○
Windows	○	○	○
Doors	○	○	○
Sprinkler System	○	○	○
Parking	○	○	○
Other	○	○	○

NOTES ABOUT THE NEIGHBORHOOD

Appearance: _____
Traffic: _____
Safety/Security: _____
Schools: _____
HOA: _____
Other: _____

ADDITIONAL NOTES: _____
_____
_____
_____
_____

AGENTS INFORMATION

Agents Name: _____
Agent Phone Number: _____
Open House: _____

OVERALL RATING: ☆ ☆ ☆ ☆ ☆

Property Address: _____

House Nickname: _____

NMLS#: _____ Price: _____

#Bedrooms: _____ #Bathrooms: _____ #Car Garage: _____

House sq/ft: _____ Lot sq/ft: _____ Age of House: _____

THE HOME

	✘	✔	♥
Exterior Condition	○	○	○
Curve Appeal	○	○	○
Floorplan	○	○	○
Kitchen	○	○	○
Family Room	○	○	○
Dining Room	○	○	○
Laundry Room	○	○	○
Master Bedroom	○	○	○
Master Bathroom	○	○	○
Extra Bedrooms	○	○	○
Extra Bathrooms	○	○	○
Closets	○	○	○
Storage Space	○	○	○
Flooring	○	○	○

THE FEATURES

	✘	✔	♥
Kitchen Cabinets	○	○	○
Kitchen Apppliances	○	○	○
Washer/Dryer	○	○	○
Fireplace	○	○	○
Patio/Balcony	○	○	○
Pool	○	○	○
Landscaping	○	○	○
A/C/Heating	○	○	○
Roof	○	○	○
Windows	○	○	○
Doors	○	○	○
Sprinkler System	○	○	○
Parking	○	○	○
Other	○	○	○

NOTES ABOUT THE NEIGHBORHOOD

Appearance: _____

Traffic: _____

Safety/Security: _____

Schools: _____

HOA: _____

Other: _____

ADDITIONAL NOTES: _____

_____
_____
_____
_____

AGENTS INFORMATION

Agents Name: _____

Agent Phone Number: _____

Open House: _____

OVERALL RATING: ☆☆☆☆☆

Property Address: _____

House Nickname: _____

NMLS#: _____   Price: _____

#Bedrooms: _____   #Bathrooms: _____   #Car Garage: _____

House sq/ft: _____   Lot sq/ft: _____   Age of House: _____

THE HOME

	✘	✔	♥
Exterior Condition	○	○	○
Curve Appeal	○	○	○
Floorplan	○	○	○
Kitchen	○	○	○
Family Room	○	○	○
Dining Room	○	○	○
Laundry Room	○	○	○
Master Bedroom	○	○	○
Master Bathroom	○	○	○
Extra Bedrooms	○	○	○
Extra Bathrooms	○	○	○
Closets	○	○	○
Storage Space	○	○	○
Flooring	○	○	○

THE FEATURES

	✘	✔	♥
Kitchen Cabinets	○	○	○
Kitchen Apppliances	○	○	○
Washer/Dryer	○	○	○
Fireplace	○	○	○
Patio/Balcony	○	○	○
Pool	○	○	○
Landscaping	○	○	○
A/C/Heating	○	○	○
Roof	○	○	○
Windows	○	○	○
Doors	○	○	○
Sprinkler System	○	○	○
Parking	○	○	○
Other	○	○	○

NOTES ABOUT THE NEIGHBORHOOD

Appearance: _____

Traffic: _____

Safety/Security: _____

Schools: _____

HOA: _____

Other: _____

ADDITIONAL NOTES: _____

_____

_____

_____

_____

AGENTS INFORMATION

Agents Name: _____

Agent Phone Number: _____

Open House: _____

OVERALL RATING: ☆ ☆ ☆ ☆ ☆

Property Address: _____

House Nickname: _____

NMLS#: _____ Price: _____

#Bedrooms: _____ #Bathrooms: _____ #Car Garage: _____

House sq/ft: _____ Lot sq/ft: _____ Age of House: _____

THE HOME

	X	✓	♥
Exterior Condition	○	○	○
Curve Appeal	○	○	○
Floorplan	○	○	○
Kitchen	○	○	○
Family Room	○	○	○
Dining Room	○	○	○
Laundry Room	○	○	○
Master Bedroom	○	○	○
Master Bathroom	○	○	○
Extra Bedrooms	○	○	○
Extra Bathrooms	○	○	○
Closets	○	○	○
Storage Space	○	○	○
Flooring	○	○	○

THE FEATURES

	X	✓	♥
Kitchen Cabinets	○	○	○
Kitchen Apppliances	○	○	○
Washer/Dryer	○	○	○
Fireplace	○	○	○
Patio/Balcony	○	○	○
Pool	○	○	○
Landscaping	○	○	○
A/C/Heating	○	○	○
Roof	○	○	○
Windows	○	○	○
Doors	○	○	○
Sprinkler System	○	○	○
Parking	○	○	○
Other	○	○	○

NOTES ABOUT THE NEIGHBORHOOD

Appearance: _____

Traffic: _____

Safety/Security: _____

Schools: _____

HOA: _____

Other: _____

ADDITIONAL NOTES: _____

_____
_____
_____
_____

AGENTS INFORMATION

Agents Name: _____

Agent Phone Number: _____

Open House: _____

OVERALL RATING: ☆ ☆ ☆ ☆ ☆

Property Address: _____
House Nickname: _____
NMLS#: _____   Price: _____
#Bedrooms: _____   #Bathrooms: _____   #Car Garage: _____
House sq/ft: _____   Lot sq/ft: _____   Age of House: _____

THE HOME

	✗	✓	♥
Exterior Condition	○	○	○
Curve Appeal	○	○	○
Floorplan	○	○	○
Kitchen	○	○	○
Family Room	○	○	○
Dining Room	○	○	○
Laundry Room	○	○	○
Master Bedroom	○	○	○
Master Bathroom	○	○	○
Extra Bedrooms	○	○	○
Extra Bathrooms	○	○	○
Closets	○	○	○
Storage Space	○	○	○
Flooring	○	○	○

THE FEATURES

	✗	✓	♥
Kitchen Cabinets	○	○	○
Kitchen Apppliances	○	○	○
Washer/Dryer	○	○	○
Fireplace	○	○	○
Patio/Balcony	○	○	○
Pool	○	○	○
Landscaping	○	○	○
A/C/Heating	○	○	○
Roof	○	○	○
Windows	○	○	○
Doors	○	○	○
Sprinkler System	○	○	○
Parking	○	○	○
Other	○	○	○

NOTES ABOUT THE NEIGHBORHOOD

Appearance: _____
Traffic: _____
Safety/Security: _____
Schools: _____
HOA: _____
Other: _____

ADDITIONAL NOTES: _____
_____
_____
_____
_____

AGENTS INFORMATION

Agents Name: _____
Agent Phone Number: _____
Open House: _____

OVERALL RATING: ☆ ☆ ☆ ☆ ☆

Property Address: _____
House Nickname: _____
NMLS#: _____ Price: _____
#Bedrooms: _____ #Bathrooms: _____ #Car Garage: _____
House sq/ft: _____ Lot sq/ft: _____ Age of House: _____

THE HOME

	X	✔	♥
Exterior Condition	○	○	○
Curve Appeal	○	○	○
Floorplan	○	○	○
Kitchen	○	○	○
Family Room	○	○	○
Dining Room	○	○	○
Laundry Room	○	○	○
Master Bedroom	○	○	○
Master Bathroom	○	○	○
Extra Bedrooms	○	○	○
Extra Bathrooms	○	○	○
Closets	○	○	○
Storage Space	○	○	○
Flooring	○	○	○

THE FEATURES

	X	✔	♥
Kitchen Cabinets	○	○	○
Kitchen Apppliances	○	○	○
Washer/Dryer	○	○	○
Fireplace	○	○	○
Patio/Balcony	○	○	○
Pool	○	○	○
Landscaping	○	○	○
A/C/Heating	○	○	○
Roof	○	○	○
Windows	○	○	○
Doors	○	○	○
Sprinkler System	○	○	○
Parking	○	○	○
Other	○	○	○

NOTES ABOUT THE NEIGHBORHOOD

Appearance: _____
Traffic: _____
Safety/Security: _____
Schools: _____
HOA: _____
Other: _____

ADDITIONAL NOTES: _____
_____
_____
_____
_____

AGENTS INFORMATION

Agents Name: _____
Agent Phone Number: _____
Open House: _____

OVERALL RATING: ☆ ☆ ☆ ☆ ☆

Property Address: _____
House Nickname: _____
NMLS#: _____ Price: _____
#Bedrooms: _____ #Bathrooms: _____ #Car Garage: _____
House sq/ft: _____ Lot sq/ft: _____ Age of House: _____

THE HOME

	X	✓	♥
Exterior Condition	○	○	○
Curve Appeal	○	○	○
Floorplan	○	○	○
Kitchen	○	○	○
Family Room	○	○	○
Dining Room	○	○	○
Laundry Room	○	○	○
Master Bedroom	○	○	○
Master Bathroom	○	○	○
Extra Bedrooms	○	○	○
Extra Bathrooms	○	○	○
Closets	○	○	○
Storage Space	○	○	○
Flooring	○	○	○

THE FEATURES

	X	✓	♥
Kitchen Cabinets	○	○	○
Kitchen Apppliances	○	○	○
Washer/Dryer	○	○	○
Fireplace	○	○	○
Patio/Balcony	○	○	○
Pool	○	○	○
Landscaping	○	○	○
A/C/Heating	○	○	○
Roof	○	○	○
Windows	○	○	○
Doors	○	○	○
Sprinkler System	○	○	○
Parking	○	○	○
Other	○	○	○

NOTES ABOUT THE NEIGHBORHOOD

Appearance: _____
Traffic: _____
Safety/Security: _____
Schools: _____
HOA: _____
Other: _____

ADDITIONAL NOTES: _____
_____
_____
_____
_____

AGENTS INFORMATION

Agents Name: _____
Agent Phone Number: _____
Open House: _____

OVERALL RATING: ☆ ☆ ☆ ☆ ☆

Property Address: _____
House Nickname: _____
NMLS#: _____ Price: _____
#Bedrooms: _____ #Bathrooms: _____ #Car Garage: _____
House sq/ft: _____ Lot sq/ft: _____ Age of House: _____

THE HOME

	X	✓	♥
Exterior Condition	○	○	○
Curve Appeal	○	○	○
Floorplan	○	○	○
Kitchen	○	○	○
Family Room	○	○	○
Dining Room	○	○	○
Laundry Room	○	○	○
Master Bedroom	○	○	○
Master Bathroom	○	○	○
Extra Bedrooms	○	○	○
Extra Bathrooms	○	○	○
Closets	○	○	○
Storage Space	○	○	○
Flooring	○	○	○

THE FEATURES

	X	✓	♥
Kitchen Cabinets	○	○	○
Kitchen Apppliances	○	○	○
Washer/Dryer	○	○	○
Fireplace	○	○	○
Patio/Balcony	○	○	○
Pool	○	○	○
Landscaping	○	○	○
A/C/Heating	○	○	○
Roof	○	○	○
Windows	○	○	○
Doors	○	○	○
Sprinkler System	○	○	○
Parking	○	○	○
Other	○	○	○

NOTES ABOUT THE NEIGHBORHOOD

Appearance: _____
Traffic: _____
Safety/Security: _____
Schools: _____
HOA: _____
Other: _____

ADDITIONAL NOTES: _____
_____
_____
_____
_____

AGENTS INFORMATION

Agents Name: _____
Agent Phone Number: _____
Open House: _____

OVERALL RATING: ☆ ☆ ☆ ☆ ☆

Property Address: _____
House Nickname: _____
NMLS#: _____   Price: _____
#Bedrooms: _____   #Bathrooms: _____   #Car Garage: _____
House sq/ft: _____   Lot sq/ft: _____   Age of House: _____

THE HOME

	X	✔	♥
Exterior Condition	○	○	○
Curve Appeal	○	○	○
Floorplan	○	○	○
Kitchen	○	○	○
Family Room	○	○	○
Dining Room	○	○	○
Laundry Room	○	○	○
Master Bedroom	○	○	○
Master Bathroom	○	○	○
Extra Bedrooms	○	○	○
Extra Bathrooms	○	○	○
Closets	○	○	○
Storage Space	○	○	○
Flooring	○	○	○

THE FEATURES

	X	✔	♥
Kitchen Cabinets	○	○	○
Kitchen Apppliances	○	○	○
Washer/Dryer	○	○	○
Fireplace	○	○	○
Patio/Balcony	○	○	○
Pool	○	○	○
Landscaping	○	○	○
A/C/Heating	○	○	○
Roof	○	○	○
Windows	○	○	○
Doors	○	○	○
Sprinkler System	○	○	○
Parking	○	○	○
Other	○	○	○

NOTES ABOUT THE NEIGHBORHOOD

Appearance: _____
Traffic: _____
Safety/Security: _____
Schools: _____
HOA: _____
Other: _____

ADDITIONAL NOTES: _____
_____
_____
_____
_____

AGENTS INFORMATION

Agents Name: _____
Agent Phone Number: _____
Open House: _____

OVERALL RATING: ☆ ☆ ☆ ☆ ☆

Property Address: _____
House Nickname: _____
NMLS#: _____ Price: _____
#Bedrooms: _____ #Bathrooms: _____ #Car Garage: _____
House sq/ft: _____ Lot sq/ft: _____ Age of House: _____

THE HOME

	X	✔	♥
Exterior Condition	◯	◯	◯
Curve Appeal	◯	◯	◯
Floorplan	◯	◯	◯
Kitchen	◯	◯	◯
Family Room	◯	◯	◯
Dining Room	◯	◯	◯
Laundry Room	◯	◯	◯
Master Bedroom	◯	◯	◯
Master Bathroom	◯	◯	◯
Extra Bedrooms	◯	◯	◯
Extra Bathrooms	◯	◯	◯
Closets	◯	◯	◯
Storage Space	◯	◯	◯
Flooring	◯	◯	◯

THE FEATURES

	X	✔	♥
Kitchen Cabinets	◯	◯	◯
Kitchen Apppliances	◯	◯	◯
Washer/Dryer	◯	◯	◯
Fireplace	◯	◯	◯
Patio/Balcony	◯	◯	◯
Pool	◯	◯	◯
Landscaping	◯	◯	◯
A/C/Heating	◯	◯	◯
Roof	◯	◯	◯
Windows	◯	◯	◯
Doors	◯	◯	◯
Sprinkler System	◯	◯	◯
Parking	◯	◯	◯
Other	◯	◯	◯

NOTES ABOUT THE NEIGHBORHOOD

Appearance: _____
Traffic: _____
Safety/Security: _____
Schools: _____
HOA: _____
Other: _____

ADDITIONAL NOTES: _____
_____
_____
_____
_____

AGENTS INFORMATION

Agents Name: _____
Agent Phone Number: _____
Open House: _____

OVERALL RATING: ☆ ☆ ☆ ☆ ☆

Property Address: _____
House Nickname: _____
NMLS#: _____ Price: _____
#Bedrooms: _____ #Bathrooms: _____ #Car Garage: _____
House sq/ft: _____ Lot sq/ft: _____ Age of House: _____

THE HOME

	X	✓	♥
Exterior Condition	○	○	○
Curve Appeal	○	○	○
Floorplan	○	○	○
Kitchen	○	○	○
Family Room	○	○	○
Dining Room	○	○	○
Laundry Room	○	○	○
Master Bedroom	○	○	○
Master Bathroom	○	○	○
Extra Bedrooms	○	○	○
Extra Bathrooms	○	○	○
Closets	○	○	○
Storage Space	○	○	○
Flooring	○	○	○

THE FEATURES

	X	✓	♥
Kitchen Cabinets	○	○	○
Kitchen Apppliances	○	○	○
Washer/Dryer	○	○	○
Fireplace	○	○	○
Patio/Balcony	○	○	○
Pool	○	○	○
Landscaping	○	○	○
A/C/Heating	○	○	○
Roof	○	○	○
Windows	○	○	○
Doors	○	○	○
Sprinkler System	○	○	○
Parking	○	○	○
Other	○	○	○

NOTES ABOUT THE NEIGHBORHOOD

Appearance: _____
Traffic: _____
Safety/Security: _____
Schools: _____
HOA: _____
Other: _____

ADDITIONAL NOTES: _____

_____
_____
_____
_____

AGENTS INFORMATION

Agents Name: _____
Agent Phone Number: _____
Open House: _____

OVERALL RATING: ☆☆☆☆☆

Property Address: _____

House Nickname: _____

NMLS#: _____ Price: _____

#Bedrooms: _____ #Bathrooms: _____ #Car Garage: _____

House sq/ft: _____ Lot sq/ft: _____ Age of House: _____

THE HOME

	X	✓	♥
Exterior Condition	◯	◯	◯
Curve Appeal	◯	◯	◯
Floorplan	◯	◯	◯
Kitchen	◯	◯	◯
Family Room	◯	◯	◯
Dining Room	◯	◯	◯
Laundry Room	◯	◯	◯
Master Bedroom	◯	◯	◯
Master Bathroom	◯	◯	◯
Extra Bedrooms	◯	◯	◯
Extra Bathrooms	◯	◯	◯
Closets	◯	◯	◯
Storage Space	◯	◯	◯
Flooring	◯	◯	◯

THE FEATURES

	X	✓	♥
Kitchen Cabinets	◯	◯	◯
Kitchen Apppliances	◯	◯	◯
Washer/Dryer	◯	◯	◯
Fireplace	◯	◯	◯
Patio/Balcony	◯	◯	◯
Pool	◯	◯	◯
Landscaping	◯	◯	◯
A/C/Heating	◯	◯	◯
Roof	◯	◯	◯
Windows	◯	◯	◯
Doors	◯	◯	◯
Sprinkler System	◯	◯	◯
Parking	◯	◯	◯
Other	◯	◯	◯

NOTES ABOUT THE NEIGHBORHOOD

Appearance: _____

Traffic: _____

Safety/Security: _____

Schools: _____

HOA: _____

Other: _____

ADDITIONAL NOTES: _____

_____

_____

_____

_____

AGENTS INFORMATION

Agents Name: _____

Agent Phone Number: _____

Open House: _____

OVERALL RATING: ☆ ☆ ☆ ☆ ☆

Property Address: _____

House Nickname: _____

NMLS#: _____   Price: _____

#Bedrooms: _____   #Bathrooms: _____   #Car Garage: _____

House sq/ft: _____   Lot sq/ft: _____   Age of House: _____

THE HOME

	X	✓	♥
Exterior Condition	○	○	○
Curve Appeal	○	○	○
Floorplan	○	○	○
Kitchen	○	○	○
Family Room	○	○	○
Dining Room	○	○	○
Laundry Room	○	○	○
Master Bedroom	○	○	○
Master Bathroom	○	○	○
Extra Bedrooms	○	○	○
Extra Bathrooms	○	○	○
Closets	○	○	○
Storage Space	○	○	○
Flooring	○	○	○

THE FEATURES

	X	✓	♥
Kitchen Cabinets	○	○	○
Kitchen Apppliances	○	○	○
Washer/Dryer	○	○	○
Fireplace	○	○	○
Patio/Balcony	○	○	○
Pool	○	○	○
Landscaping	○	○	○
A/C/Heating	○	○	○
Roof	○	○	○
Windows	○	○	○
Doors	○	○	○
Sprinkler System	○	○	○
Parking	○	○	○
Other	○	○	○

NOTES ABOUT THE NEIGHBORHOOD

Appearance: _____

Traffic: _____

Safety/Security: _____

Schools: _____

HOA: _____

Other: _____

ADDITIONAL NOTES: _____

_____

_____

_____

_____

AGENTS INFORMATION

Agents Name: _____

Agent Phone Number: _____

Open House: _____

OVERALL RATING: ☆ ☆ ☆ ☆ ☆

Property Address: _____

House Nickname: _____

NMLS#: _____   Price: _____

#Bedrooms: _____   #Bathrooms: _____   #Car Garage: _____

House sq/ft: _____   Lot sq/ft: _____   Age of House: _____

THE HOME

	✘	✔	♥
Exterior Condition	○	○	○
Curve Appeal	○	○	○
Floorplan	○	○	○
Kitchen	○	○	○
Family Room	○	○	○
Dining Room	○	○	○
Laundry Room	○	○	○
Master Bedroom	○	○	○
Master Bathroom	○	○	○
Extra Bedrooms	○	○	○
Extra Bathrooms	○	○	○
Closets	○	○	○
Storage Space	○	○	○
Flooring	○	○	○

THE FEATURES

	✘	✔	♥
Kitchen Cabinets	○	○	○
Kitchen Apppliances	○	○	○
Washer/Dryer	○	○	○
Fireplace	○	○	○
Patio/Balcony	○	○	○
Pool	○	○	○
Landscaping	○	○	○
A/C/Heating	○	○	○
Roof	○	○	○
Windows	○	○	○
Doors	○	○	○
Sprinkler System	○	○	○
Parking	○	○	○
Other	○	○	○

NOTES ABOUT THE NEIGHBORHOOD

Appearance: _____

Traffic: _____

Safety/Security: _____

Schools: _____

HOA: _____

Other: _____

ADDITIONAL NOTES: _____

_____

_____

_____

_____

AGENTS INFORMATION

Agents Name: _____

Agent Phone Number: _____

Open House: _____

OVERALL RATING: ☆ ☆ ☆ ☆ ☆

Property Address: _____
House Nickname: _____
NMLS#: _____ Price: _____
#Bedrooms: _____ #Bathrooms: _____ #Car Garage: _____
House sq/ft: _____ Lot sq/ft: _____ Age of House: _____

THE HOME

	X	✓	♥
Exterior Condition	○	○	○
Curve Appeal	○	○	○
Floorplan	○	○	○
Kitchen	○	○	○
Family Room	○	○	○
Dining Room	○	○	○
Laundry Room	○	○	○
Master Bedroom	○	○	○
Master Bathroom	○	○	○
Extra Bedrooms	○	○	○
Extra Bathrooms	○	○	○
Closets	○	○	○
Storage Space	○	○	○
Flooring	○	○	○

THE FEATURES

	X	✓	♥
Kitchen Cabinets	○	○	○
Kitchen Apppliances	○	○	○
Washer/Dryer	○	○	○
Fireplace	○	○	○
Patio/Balcony	○	○	○
Pool	○	○	○
Landscaping	○	○	○
A/C/Heating	○	○	○
Roof	○	○	○
Windows	○	○	○
Doors	○	○	○
Sprinkler System	○	○	○
Parking	○	○	○
Other	○	○	○

NOTES ABOUT THE NEIGHBORHOOD

Appearance: _____
Traffic: _____
Safety/Security: _____
Schools: _____
HOA: _____
Other: _____

ADDITIONAL NOTES: _____
_____
_____
_____
_____

AGENTS INFORMATION

Agents Name: _____
Agent Phone Number: _____
Open House: _____

OVERALL RATING: ☆☆☆☆☆

Property Address: _____
House Nickname: _____
NMLS#: _____ Price: _____
#Bedrooms: _____ #Bathrooms: _____ #Car Garage: _____
House sq/ft: _____ Lot sq/ft: _____ Age of House: _____

THE HOME

	X	✓	♥
Exterior Condition	○	○	○
Curve Appeal	○	○	○
Floorplan	○	○	○
Kitchen	○	○	○
Family Room	○	○	○
Dining Room	○	○	○
Laundry Room	○	○	○
Master Bedroom	○	○	○
Master Bathroom	○	○	○
Extra Bedrooms	○	○	○
Extra Bathrooms	○	○	○
Closets	○	○	○
Storage Space	○	○	○
Flooring	○	○	○

THE FEATURES

	X	✓	♥
Kitchen Cabinets	○	○	○
Kitchen Apppliances	○	○	○
Washer/Dryer	○	○	○
Fireplace	○	○	○
Patio/Balcony	○	○	○
Pool	○	○	○
Landscaping	○	○	○
A/C/Heating	○	○	○
Roof	○	○	○
Windows	○	○	○
Doors	○	○	○
Sprinkler System	○	○	○
Parking	○	○	○
Other	○	○	○

NOTES ABOUT THE NEIGHBORHOOD

Appearance: _____
Traffic: _____
Safety/Security: _____
Schools: _____
HOA: _____
Other: _____

ADDITIONAL NOTES: _____
_____
_____
_____
_____

AGENTS INFORMATION

Agents Name: _____
Agent Phone Number: _____
Open House: _____

OVERALL RATING: ☆ ☆ ☆ ☆ ☆

Property Address: _____

House Nickname: _____

NMLS#: _____ Price: _____

#Bedrooms: _____ #Bathrooms: _____ #Car Garage: _____

House sq/ft: _____ Lot sq/ft: _____ Age of House: _____

THE HOME

	✖	✔	♥
Exterior Condition	○	○	○
Curve Appeal	○	○	○
Floorplan	○	○	○
Kitchen	○	○	○
Family Room	○	○	○
Dining Room	○	○	○
Laundry Room	○	○	○
Master Bedroom	○	○	○
Master Bathroom	○	○	○
Extra Bedrooms	○	○	○
Extra Bathrooms	○	○	○
Closets	○	○	○
Storage Space	○	○	○
Flooring	○	○	○

THE FEATURES

	✖	✔	♥
Kitchen Cabinets	○	○	○
Kitchen Apppliances	○	○	○
Washer/Dryer	○	○	○
Fireplace	○	○	○
Patio/Balcony	○	○	○
Pool	○	○	○
Landscaping	○	○	○
A/C/Heating	○	○	○
Roof	○	○	○
Windows	○	○	○
Doors	○	○	○
Sprinkler System	○	○	○
Parking	○	○	○
Other	○	○	○

NOTES ABOUT THE NEIGHBORHOOD

Appearance: _____

Traffic: _____

Safety/Security: _____

Schools: _____

HOA: _____

Other: _____

ADDITIONAL NOTES: _____

_____

_____

_____

_____

AGENTS INFORMATION

Agents Name: _____

Agent Phone Number: _____

Open House: _____

OVERALL RATING: ☆ ☆ ☆ ☆ ☆

Property Address: _____

House Nickname: _____

NMLS#: _____ Price: _____

#Bedrooms: _____ #Bathrooms: _____ #Car Garage: _____

House sq/ft: _____ Lot sq/ft: _____ Age of House: _____

THE HOME

	X	✓	♥
Exterior Condition	○	○	○
Curve Appeal	○	○	○
Floorplan	○	○	○
Kitchen	○	○	○
Family Room	○	○	○
Dining Room	○	○	○
Laundry Room	○	○	○
Master Bedroom	○	○	○
Master Bathroom	○	○	○
Extra Bedrooms	○	○	○
Extra Bathrooms	○	○	○
Closets	○	○	○
Storage Space	○	○	○
Flooring	○	○	○

THE FEATURES

	X	✓	♥
Kitchen Cabinets	○	○	○
Kitchen Apppliances	○	○	○
Washer/Dryer	○	○	○
Fireplace	○	○	○
Patio/Balcony	○	○	○
Pool	○	○	○
Landscaping	○	○	○
A/C/Heating	○	○	○
Roof	○	○	○
Windows	○	○	○
Doors	○	○	○
Sprinkler System	○	○	○
Parking	○	○	○
Other	○	○	○

NOTES ABOUT THE NEIGHBORHOOD

Appearance: _____

Traffic: _____

Safety/Security: _____

Schools: _____

HOA: _____

Other: _____

ADDITIONAL NOTES: _____

_____

_____

_____

_____

AGENTS INFORMATION

Agents Name: _____

Agent Phone Number: _____

Open House: _____

OVERALL RATING: ☆ ☆ ☆ ☆ ☆

Property Address: _____
House Nickname: _____
NMLS#: _____   Price: _____
#Bedrooms: _____   #Bathrooms: _____   #Car Garage: _____
House sq/ft: _____   Lot sq/ft: _____   Age of House: _____

THE HOME

	X	✓	♥
Exterior Condition	○	○	○
Curve Appeal	○	○	○
Floorplan	○	○	○
Kitchen	○	○	○
Family Room	○	○	○
Dining Room	○	○	○
Laundry Room	○	○	○
Master Bedroom	○	○	○
Master Bathroom	○	○	○
Extra Bedrooms	○	○	○
Extra Bathrooms	○	○	○
Closets	○	○	○
Storage Space	○	○	○
Flooring	○	○	○

THE FEATURES

	X	✓	♥
Kitchen Cabinets	○	○	○
Kitchen Apppliances	○	○	○
Washer/Dryer	○	○	○
Fireplace	○	○	○
Patio/Balcony	○	○	○
Pool	○	○	○
Landscaping	○	○	○
A/C/Heating	○	○	○
Roof	○	○	○
Windows	○	○	○
Doors	○	○	○
Sprinkler System	○	○	○
Parking	○	○	○
Other	○	○	○

NOTES ABOUT THE NEIGHBORHOOD

Appearance: _____
Traffic: _____
Safety/Security: _____
Schools: _____
HOA: _____
Other: _____

ADDITIONAL NOTES: _____
_____
_____
_____
_____

AGENTS INFORMATION

Agents Name: _____
Agent Phone Number: _____
Open House: _____

OVERALL RATING: ☆ ☆ ☆ ☆ ☆

Property Address: _____
House Nickname: _____
NMLS#: _____ **Price:** _____
#Bedrooms: _____ **#Bathrooms:** _____ **#Car Garage:** _____
House sq/ft: _____ **Lot sq/ft:** _____ **Age of House:** _____

THE HOME

	X	✓	♥
Exterior Condition	○	○	○
Curve Appeal	○	○	○
Floorplan	○	○	○
Kitchen	○	○	○
Family Room	○	○	○
Dining Room	○	○	○
Laundry Room	○	○	○
Master Bedroom	○	○	○
Master Bathroom	○	○	○
Extra Bedrooms	○	○	○
Extra Bathrooms	○	○	○
Closets	○	○	○
Storage Space	○	○	○
Flooring	○	○	○

THE FEATURES

	X	✓	♥
Kitchen Cabinets	○	○	○
Kitchen Apppliances	○	○	○
Washer/Dryer	○	○	○
Fireplace	○	○	○
Patio/Balcony	○	○	○
Pool	○	○	○
Landscaping	○	○	○
A/C/Heating	○	○	○
Roof	○	○	○
Windows	○	○	○
Doors	○	○	○
Sprinkler System	○	○	○
Parking	○	○	○
Other	○	○	○

NOTES ABOUT THE NEIGHBORHOOD

Appearance: _____
Traffic: _____
Safety/Security: _____
Schools: _____
HOA: _____
Other: _____

ADDITIONAL NOTES: _____
_____
_____
_____
_____

AGENTS INFORMATION

Agents Name: _____
Agent Phone Number: _____
Open House: _____

OVERALL RATING: ☆ ☆ ☆ ☆ ☆

Property Address: _____

House Nickname: _____

NMLS#: _____   Price: _____

#Bedrooms: _____   #Bathrooms: _____   #Car Garage: _____

House sq/ft: _____   Lot sq/ft: _____   Age of House: _____

THE HOME

	X	✓	♥
Exterior Condition	○	○	○
Curve Appeal	○	○	○
Floorplan	○	○	○
Kitchen	○	○	○
Family Room	○	○	○
Dining Room	○	○	○
Laundry Room	○	○	○
Master Bedroom	○	○	○
Master Bathroom	○	○	○
Extra Bedrooms	○	○	○
Extra Bathrooms	○	○	○
Closets	○	○	○
Storage Space	○	○	○
Flooring	○	○	○

THE FEATURES

	X	✓	♥
Kitchen Cabinets	○	○	○
Kitchen Apppliances	○	○	○
Washer/Dryer	○	○	○
Fireplace	○	○	○
Patio/Balcony	○	○	○
Pool	○	○	○
Landscaping	○	○	○
A/C/Heating	○	○	○
Roof	○	○	○
Windows	○	○	○
Doors	○	○	○
Sprinkler System	○	○	○
Parking	○	○	○
Other	○	○	○

NOTES ABOUT THE NEIGHBORHOOD

Appearance: _____

Traffic: _____

Safety/Security: _____

Schools: _____

HOA: _____

Other: _____

ADDITIONAL NOTES: _____

_____

_____

_____

_____

AGENTS INFORMATION

Agents Name: _____

Agent Phone Number: _____

Open House: _____

OVERALL RATING: ☆ ☆ ☆ ☆ ☆

Property Address: _____

House Nickname: _____

NMLS#: _____ Price: _____

#Bedrooms: _____ #Bathrooms: _____ #Car Garage: _____

House sq/ft: _____ Lot sq/ft: _____ Age of House: _____

THE HOME

	✗	✓	♥
Exterior Condition	○	○	○
Curve Appeal	○	○	○
Floorplan	○	○	○
Kitchen	○	○	○
Family Room	○	○	○
Dining Room	○	○	○
Laundry Room	○	○	○
Master Bedroom	○	○	○
Master Bathroom	○	○	○
Extra Bedrooms	○	○	○
Extra Bathrooms	○	○	○
Closets	○	○	○
Storage Space	○	○	○
Flooring	○	○	○

THE FEATURES

	✗	✓	♥
Kitchen Cabinets	○	○	○
Kitchen Apppliances	○	○	○
Washer/Dryer	○	○	○
Fireplace	○	○	○
Patio/Balcony	○	○	○
Pool	○	○	○
Landscaping	○	○	○
A/C/Heating	○	○	○
Roof	○	○	○
Windows	○	○	○
Doors	○	○	○
Sprinkler System	○	○	○
Parking	○	○	○
Other	○	○	○

NOTES ABOUT THE NEIGHBORHOOD

Appearance: _____

Traffic: _____

Safety/Security: _____

Schools: _____

HOA: _____

Other: _____

ADDITIONAL NOTES: _____

_____

_____

_____

_____

AGENTS INFORMATION

Agents Name: _____

Agent Phone Number: _____

Open House: _____

OVERALL RATING: ☆☆☆☆☆

Property Address: _____

House Nickname: _____

NMLS#: _____ Price: _____

#Bedrooms: _____ #Bathrooms: _____ #Car Garage: _____

House sq/ft: _____ Lot sq/ft: _____ Age of House: _____

THE HOME

	✗	✓	♥
Exterior Condition	○	○	○
Curve Appeal	○	○	○
Floorplan	○	○	○
Kitchen	○	○	○
Family Room	○	○	○
Dining Room	○	○	○
Laundry Room	○	○	○
Master Bedroom	○	○	○
Master Bathroom	○	○	○
Extra Bedrooms	○	○	○
Extra Bathrooms	○	○	○
Closets	○	○	○
Storage Space	○	○	○
Flooring	○	○	○

THE FEATURES

	✗	✓	♥
Kitchen Cabinets	○	○	○
Kitchen Apppliances	○	○	○
Washer/Dryer	○	○	○
Fireplace	○	○	○
Patio/Balcony	○	○	○
Pool	○	○	○
Landscaping	○	○	○
A/C/Heating	○	○	○
Roof	○	○	○
Windows	○	○	○
Doors	○	○	○
Sprinkler System	○	○	○
Parking	○	○	○
Other	○	○	○

NOTES ABOUT THE NEIGHBORHOOD

Appearance: _____

Traffic: _____

Safety/Security: _____

Schools: _____

HOA: _____

Other: _____

ADDITIONAL NOTES: _____

_____

_____

_____

_____

AGENTS INFORMATION

Agents Name: _____

Agent Phone Number: _____

Open House: _____

OVERALL RATING: ☆☆☆☆☆

Property Address: _____

House Nickname: _____

NMLS#: _____ Price: _____

#Bedrooms: _____ #Bathrooms: _____ #Car Garage: _____

House sq/ft: _____ Lot sq/ft: _____ Age of House: _____

THE HOME

	X	✔	♥
Exterior Condition	○	○	○
Curve Appeal	○	○	○
Floorplan	○	○	○
Kitchen	○	○	○
Family Room	○	○	○
Dining Room	○	○	○
Laundry Room	○	○	○
Master Bedroom	○	○	○
Master Bathroom	○	○	○
Extra Bedrooms	○	○	○
Extra Bathrooms	○	○	○
Closets	○	○	○
Storage Space	○	○	○
Flooring	○	○	○

THE FEATURES

	X	✔	♥
Kitchen Cabinets	○	○	○
Kitchen Apppliances	○	○	○
Washer/Dryer	○	○	○
Fireplace	○	○	○
Patio/Balcony	○	○	○
Pool	○	○	○
Landscaping	○	○	○
A/C/Heating	○	○	○
Roof	○	○	○
Windows	○	○	○
Doors	○	○	○
Sprinkler System	○	○	○
Parking	○	○	○
Other	○	○	○

NOTES ABOUT THE NEIGHBORHOOD

Appearance: _____

Traffic: _____

Safety/Security: _____

Schools: _____

HOA: _____

Other: _____

ADDITIONAL NOTES: _____

_____

_____

_____

_____

AGENTS INFORMATION

Agents Name: _____

Agent Phone Number: _____

Open House: _____

OVERALL RATING: ☆ ☆ ☆ ☆ ☆

Property Address: _____
House Nickname: _____
NMLS#: _____   Price: _____
#Bedrooms: _____   #Bathrooms: _____   #Car Garage: _____
House sq/ft: _____   Lot sq/ft: _____   Age of House: _____

THE HOME

	X	✔	♥
Exterior Condition	○	○	○
Curve Appeal	○	○	○
Floorplan	○	○	○
Kitchen	○	○	○
Family Room	○	○	○
Dining Room	○	○	○
Laundry Room	○	○	○
Master Bedroom	○	○	○
Master Bathroom	○	○	○
Extra Bedrooms	○	○	○
Extra Bathrooms	○	○	○
Closets	○	○	○
Storage Space	○	○	○
Flooring	○	○	○

THE FEATURES

	X	✔	♥
Kitchen Cabinets	○	○	○
Kitchen Apppliances	○	○	○
Washer/Dryer	○	○	○
Fireplace	○	○	○
Patio/Balcony	○	○	○
Pool	○	○	○
Landscaping	○	○	○
A/C/Heating	○	○	○
Roof	○	○	○
Windows	○	○	○
Doors	○	○	○
Sprinkler System	○	○	○
Parking	○	○	○
Other	○	○	○

NOTES ABOUT THE NEIGHBORHOOD

Appearance: _____
Traffic: _____
Safety/Security: _____
Schools: _____
HOA: _____
Other: _____

ADDITIONAL NOTES: _____

_____
_____
_____
_____

AGENTS INFORMATION

Agents Name: _____
Agent Phone Number: _____
Open House: _____

OVERALL RATING: ☆☆☆☆☆

Property Address: _____

House Nickname: _____

NMLS#: _____   Price: _____

#Bedrooms: _____   #Bathrooms: _____   #Car Garage: _____

House sq/ft: _____   Lot sq/ft: _____   Age of House: _____

THE HOME

	X	✓	♥
Exterior Condition	○	○	○
Curve Appeal	○	○	○
Floorplan	○	○	○
Kitchen	○	○	○
Family Room	○	○	○
Dining Room	○	○	○
Laundry Room	○	○	○
Master Bedroom	○	○	○
Master Bathroom	○	○	○
Extra Bedrooms	○	○	○
Extra Bathrooms	○	○	○
Closets	○	○	○
Storage Space	○	○	○
Flooring	○	○	○

THE FEATURES

	X	✓	♥
Kitchen Cabinets	○	○	○
Kitchen Apppliances	○	○	○
Washer/Dryer	○	○	○
Fireplace	○	○	○
Patio/Balcony	○	○	○
Pool	○	○	○
Landscaping	○	○	○
A/C/Heating	○	○	○
Roof	○	○	○
Windows	○	○	○
Doors	○	○	○
Sprinkler System	○	○	○
Parking	○	○	○
Other	○	○	○

NOTES ABOUT THE NEIGHBORHOOD

Appearance: _____

Traffic: _____

Safety/Security: _____

Schools: _____

HOA: _____

Other: _____

ADDITIONAL NOTES: _____

_____

_____

_____

_____

AGENTS INFORMATION

Agents Name: _____

Agent Phone Number: _____

Open House: _____

OVERALL RATING: ☆ ☆ ☆ ☆ ☆

Property Address: _____

House Nickname: _____

NMLS#: _____   Price: _____

#Bedrooms: _____   #Bathrooms: _____   #Car Garage: _____

House sq/ft: _____   Lot sq/ft: _____   Age of House: _____

THE HOME

	X	✓	♥
Exterior Condition	○	○	○
Curve Appeal	○	○	○
Floorplan	○	○	○
Kitchen	○	○	○
Family Room	○	○	○
Dining Room	○	○	○
Laundry Room	○	○	○
Master Bedroom	○	○	○
Master Bathroom	○	○	○
Extra Bedrooms	○	○	○
Extra Bathrooms	○	○	○
Closets	○	○	○
Storage Space	○	○	○
Flooring	○	○	○

THE FEATURES

	X	✓	♥
Kitchen Cabinets	○	○	○
Kitchen Apppliances	○	○	○
Washer/Dryer	○	○	○
Fireplace	○	○	○
Patio/Balcony	○	○	○
Pool	○	○	○
Landscaping	○	○	○
A/C/Heating	○	○	○
Roof	○	○	○
Windows	○	○	○
Doors	○	○	○
Sprinkler System	○	○	○
Parking	○	○	○
Other	○	○	○

NOTES ABOUT THE NEIGHBORHOOD

Appearance: _____

Traffic: _____

Safety/Security: _____

Schools: _____

HOA: _____

Other: _____

ADDITIONAL NOTES: _____

_____

_____

_____

_____

AGENTS INFORMATION

Agents Name: _____

Agent Phone Number: _____

Open House: _____

OVERALL RATING: ☆ ☆ ☆ ☆ ☆

Property Address: _____
House Nickname: _____
NMLS#: _____ Price: _____
#Bedrooms: _____ #Bathrooms: _____ #Car Garage: _____
House sq/ft: _____ Lot sq/ft: _____ Age of House: _____

THE HOME

	X	✓	♥
Exterior Condition	○	○	○
Curve Appeal	○	○	○
Floorplan	○	○	○
Kitchen	○	○	○
Family Room	○	○	○
Dining Room	○	○	○
Laundry Room	○	○	○
Master Bedroom	○	○	○
Master Bathroom	○	○	○
Extra Bedrooms	○	○	○
Extra Bathrooms	○	○	○
Closets	○	○	○
Storage Space	○	○	○
Flooring	○	○	○

THE FEATURES

	X	✓	♥
Kitchen Cabinets	○	○	○
Kitchen Apppliances	○	○	○
Washer/Dryer	○	○	○
Fireplace	○	○	○
Patio/Balcony	○	○	○
Pool	○	○	○
Landscaping	○	○	○
A/C/Heating	○	○	○
Roof	○	○	○
Windows	○	○	○
Doors	○	○	○
Sprinkler System	○	○	○
Parking	○	○	○
Other	○	○	○

NOTES ABOUT THE NEIGHBORHOOD

Appearance: _____
Traffic: _____
Safety/Security: _____
Schools: _____
HOA: _____
Other: _____

ADDITIONAL NOTES: _____
_____
_____
_____
_____

AGENTS INFORMATION

Agents Name: _____
Agent Phone Number: _____
Open House: _____

OVERALL RATING: ☆☆☆☆☆

Property Address: _____
House Nickname: _____
NMLS#: _____ Price: _____
#Bedrooms: _____ #Bathrooms: _____ #Car Garage: _____
House sq/ft: _____ Lot sq/ft: _____ Age of House: _____

THE HOME

	✗	✓	♥
Exterior Condition	○	○	○
Curve Appeal	○	○	○
Floorplan	○	○	○
Kitchen	○	○	○
Family Room	○	○	○
Dining Room	○	○	○
Laundry Room	○	○	○
Master Bedroom	○	○	○
Master Bathroom	○	○	○
Extra Bedrooms	○	○	○
Extra Bathrooms	○	○	○
Closets	○	○	○
Storage Space	○	○	○
Flooring	○	○	○

THE FEATURES

	✗	✓	♥
Kitchen Cabinets	○	○	○
Kitchen Apppliances	○	○	○
Washer/Dryer	○	○	○
Fireplace	○	○	○
Patio/Balcony	○	○	○
Pool	○	○	○
Landscaping	○	○	○
A/C/Heating	○	○	○
Roof	○	○	○
Windows	○	○	○
Doors	○	○	○
Sprinkler System	○	○	○
Parking	○	○	○
Other	○	○	○

NOTES ABOUT THE NEIGHBORHOOD

Appearance: _____
Traffic: _____
Safety/Security: _____
Schools: _____
HOA: _____
Other: _____

ADDITIONAL NOTES: _____

_____
_____
_____
_____

AGENTS INFORMATION

Agents Name: _____
Agent Phone Number: _____
Open House: _____

OVERALL RATING: ☆☆☆☆☆

Property Address: _____
House Nickname: _____
NMLS#: _____ Price: _____
#Bedrooms: _____ #Bathrooms: _____ #Car Garage: _____
House sq/ft: _____ Lot sq/ft: _____ Age of House: _____

THE HOME

	✗	✓	♥
Exterior Condition	○	○	○
Curve Appeal	○	○	○
Floorplan	○	○	○
Kitchen	○	○	○
Family Room	○	○	○
Dining Room	○	○	○
Laundry Room	○	○	○
Master Bedroom	○	○	○
Master Bathroom	○	○	○
Extra Bedrooms	○	○	○
Extra Bathrooms	○	○	○
Closets	○	○	○
Storage Space	○	○	○
Flooring	○	○	○

THE FEATURES

	✗	✓	♥
Kitchen Cabinets	○	○	○
Kitchen Apppliances	○	○	○
Washer/Dryer	○	○	○
Fireplace	○	○	○
Patio/Balcony	○	○	○
Pool	○	○	○
Landscaping	○	○	○
A/C/Heating	○	○	○
Roof	○	○	○
Windows	○	○	○
Doors	○	○	○
Sprinkler System	○	○	○
Parking	○	○	○
Other	○	○	○

NOTES ABOUT THE NEIGHBORHOOD

Appearance: _____
Traffic: _____
Safety/Security: _____
Schools: _____
HOA: _____
Other: _____

ADDITIONAL NOTES: _____
_____
_____
_____
_____

AGENTS INFORMATION

Agents Name: _____
Agent Phone Number: _____
Open House: _____

OVERALL RATING: ☆ ☆ ☆ ☆ ☆

Property Address: _____

House Nickname: _____

NMLS#: _____ Price: _____

#Bedrooms: _____ #Bathrooms: _____ #Car Garage: _____

House sq/ft: _____ Lot sq/ft: _____ Age of House: _____

THE HOME

	✗	✓	♥
Exterior Condition	○	○	○
Curve Appeal	○	○	○
Floorplan	○	○	○
Kitchen	○	○	○
Family Room	○	○	○
Dining Room	○	○	○
Laundry Room	○	○	○
Master Bedroom	○	○	○
Master Bathroom	○	○	○
Extra Bedrooms	○	○	○
Extra Bathrooms	○	○	○
Closets	○	○	○
Storage Space	○	○	○
Flooring	○	○	○

THE FEATURES

	✗	✓	♥
Kitchen Cabinets	○	○	○
Kitchen Apppliances	○	○	○
Washer/Dryer	○	○	○
Fireplace	○	○	○
Patio/Balcony	○	○	○
Pool	○	○	○
Landscaping	○	○	○
A/C/Heating	○	○	○
Roof	○	○	○
Windows	○	○	○
Doors	○	○	○
Sprinkler System	○	○	○
Parking	○	○	○
Other	○	○	○

NOTES ABOUT THE NEIGHBORHOOD

Appearance: _____

Traffic: _____

Safety/Security: _____

Schools: _____

HOA: _____

Other: _____

ADDITIONAL NOTES: _____

_____

_____

_____

_____

AGENTS INFORMATION

Agents Name: _____

Agent Phone Number: _____

Open House: _____

OVERALL RATING: ☆ ☆ ☆ ☆ ☆

Property Address: _____
House Nickname: _____
NMLS#: _____ Price: _____
#Bedrooms: _____ #Bathrooms: _____ #Car Garage: _____
House sq/ft: _____ Lot sq/ft: _____ Age of House: _____

THE HOME

	X	✓	♥
Exterior Condition	○	○	○
Curve Appeal	○	○	○
Floorplan	○	○	○
Kitchen	○	○	○
Family Room	○	○	○
Dining Room	○	○	○
Laundry Room	○	○	○
Master Bedroom	○	○	○
Master Bathroom	○	○	○
Extra Bedrooms	○	○	○
Extra Bathrooms	○	○	○
Closets	○	○	○
Storage Space	○	○	○
Flooring	○	○	○

THE FEATURES

	X	✓	♥
Kitchen Cabinets	○	○	○
Kitchen Apppliances	○	○	○
Washer/Dryer	○	○	○
Fireplace	○	○	○
Patio/Balcony	○	○	○
Pool	○	○	○
Landscaping	○	○	○
A/C/Heating	○	○	○
Roof	○	○	○
Windows	○	○	○
Doors	○	○	○
Sprinkler System	○	○	○
Parking	○	○	○
Other	○	○	○

NOTES ABOUT THE NEIGHBORHOOD

Appearance: _____
Traffic: _____
Safety/Security: _____
Schools: _____
HOA: _____
Other: _____

ADDITIONAL NOTES: _____
_____
_____
_____
_____

AGENTS INFORMATION

Agents Name: _____
Agent Phone Number: _____
Open House: _____

OVERALL RATING: ☆☆☆☆☆

Property Address: _____
House Nickname: _____
NMLS#: _____ Price: _____
#Bedrooms: _____ #Bathrooms: _____ #Car Garage: _____
House sq/ft: _____ Lot sq/ft: _____ Age of House: _____

THE HOME

	X	✓	♥
Exterior Condition	○	○	○
Curve Appeal	○	○	○
Floorplan	○	○	○
Kitchen	○	○	○
Family Room	○	○	○
Dining Room	○	○	○
Laundry Room	○	○	○
Master Bedroom	○	○	○
Master Bathroom	○	○	○
Extra Bedrooms	○	○	○
Extra Bathrooms	○	○	○
Closets	○	○	○
Storage Space	○	○	○
Flooring	○	○	○

THE FEATURES

	X	✓	♥
Kitchen Cabinets	○	○	○
Kitchen Apppliances	○	○	○
Washer/Dryer	○	○	○
Fireplace	○	○	○
Patio/Balcony	○	○	○
Pool	○	○	○
Landscaping	○	○	○
A/C/Heating	○	○	○
Roof	○	○	○
Windows	○	○	○
Doors	○	○	○
Sprinkler System	○	○	○
Parking	○	○	○
Other	○	○	○

NOTES ABOUT THE NEIGHBORHOOD

Appearance: _____
Traffic: _____
Safety/Security: _____
Schools: _____
HOA: _____
Other: _____

ADDITIONAL NOTES: _____
_____
_____
_____
_____

AGENTS INFORMATION

Agents Name: _____
Agent Phone Number: _____
Open House: _____

OVERALL RATING: ☆☆☆☆☆

Property Address: _____

House Nickname: _____

NMLS#: _____ Price: _____

#Bedrooms: _____ #Bathrooms: _____ #Car Garage: _____

House sq/ft: _____ Lot sq/ft: _____ Age of House: _____

THE HOME

	✗	✓	♥
Exterior Condition	○	○	○
Curve Appeal	○	○	○
Floorplan	○	○	○
Kitchen	○	○	○
Family Room	○	○	○
Dining Room	○	○	○
Laundry Room	○	○	○
Master Bedroom	○	○	○
Master Bathroom	○	○	○
Extra Bedrooms	○	○	○
Extra Bathrooms	○	○	○
Closets	○	○	○
Storage Space	○	○	○
Flooring	○	○	○

THE FEATURES

	✗	✓	♥
Kitchen Cabinets	○	○	○
Kitchen Apppliances	○	○	○
Washer/Dryer	○	○	○
Fireplace	○	○	○
Patio/Balcony	○	○	○
Pool	○	○	○
Landscaping	○	○	○
A/C/Heating	○	○	○
Roof	○	○	○
Windows	○	○	○
Doors	○	○	○
Sprinkler System	○	○	○
Parking	○	○	○
Other	○	○	○

NOTES ABOUT THE NEIGHBORHOOD

Appearance: _____

Traffic: _____

Safety/Security: _____

Schools: _____

HOA: _____

Other: _____

ADDITIONAL NOTES: _____

_____

_____

_____

_____

AGENTS INFORMATION

Agents Name: _____

Agent Phone Number: _____

Open House: _____

OVERALL RATING: ☆ ☆ ☆ ☆ ☆

Property Address: _____

House Nickname: _____

NMLS#: _____ Price: _____

#Bedrooms: _____ #Bathrooms: _____ #Car Garage: _____

House sq/ft: _____ Lot sq/ft: _____ Age of House: _____

THE HOME

	X	**✓**	**♥**
Exterior Condition	○	○	○
Curve Appeal	○	○	○
Floorplan	○	○	○
Kitchen	○	○	○
Family Room	○	○	○
Dining Room	○	○	○
Laundry Room	○	○	○
Master Bedroom	○	○	○
Master Bathroom	○	○	○
Extra Bedrooms	○	○	○
Extra Bathrooms	○	○	○
Closets	○	○	○
Storage Space	○	○	○
Flooring	○	○	○

THE FEATURES

	X	**✓**	**♥**
Kitchen Cabinets	○	○	○
Kitchen Apppliances	○	○	○
Washer/Dryer	○	○	○
Fireplace	○	○	○
Patio/Balcony	○	○	○
Pool	○	○	○
Landscaping	○	○	○
A/C/Heating	○	○	○
Roof	○	○	○
Windows	○	○	○
Doors	○	○	○
Sprinkler System	○	○	○
Parking	○	○	○
Other	○	○	○

NOTES ABOUT THE NEIGHBORHOOD

Appearance: _____

Traffic: _____

Safety/Security: _____

Schools: _____

HOA: _____

Other: _____

ADDITIONAL NOTES: _____

_____

_____

_____

_____

AGENTS INFORMATION

Agents Name: _____

Agent Phone Number: _____

Open House: _____

OVERALL RATING: ☆☆☆☆☆

Property Address: _____

House Nickname: _____

NMLS#: _____   Price: _____

#Bedrooms: _____   #Bathrooms: _____   #Car Garage: _____

House sq/ft: _____   Lot sq/ft: _____   Age of House: _____

THE HOME

	X	✓	♥
Exterior Condition	○	○	○
Curve Appeal	○	○	○
Floorplan	○	○	○
Kitchen	○	○	○
Family Room	○	○	○
Dining Room	○	○	○
Laundry Room	○	○	○
Master Bedroom	○	○	○
Master Bathroom	○	○	○
Extra Bedrooms	○	○	○
Extra Bathrooms	○	○	○
Closets	○	○	○
Storage Space	○	○	○
Flooring	○	○	○

THE FEATURES

	X	✓	♥
Kitchen Cabinets	○	○	○
Kitchen Apppliances	○	○	○
Washer/Dryer	○	○	○
Fireplace	○	○	○
Patio/Balcony	○	○	○
Pool	○	○	○
Landscaping	○	○	○
A/C/Heating	○	○	○
Roof	○	○	○
Windows	○	○	○
Doors	○	○	○
Sprinkler System	○	○	○
Parking	○	○	○
Other	○	○	○

NOTES ABOUT THE NEIGHBORHOOD

Appearance: _____

Traffic: _____

Safety/Security: _____

Schools: _____

HOA: _____

Other: _____

ADDITIONAL NOTES: _____

_____

_____

_____

_____

AGENTS INFORMATION

Agents Name: _____

Agent Phone Number: _____

Open House: _____

OVERALL RATING: ☆ ☆ ☆ ☆ ☆

Property Address: _____

House Nickname: _____

NMLS#: _____ Price: _____

#Bedrooms: _____ #Bathrooms: _____ #Car Garage: _____

House sq/ft: _____ Lot sq/ft: _____ Age of House: _____

THE HOME

	✗	✓	♥
Exterior Condition	○	○	○
Curve Appeal	○	○	○
Floorplan	○	○	○
Kitchen	○	○	○
Family Room	○	○	○
Dining Room	○	○	○
Laundry Room	○	○	○
Master Bedroom	○	○	○
Master Bathroom	○	○	○
Extra Bedrooms	○	○	○
Extra Bathrooms	○	○	○
Closets	○	○	○
Storage Space	○	○	○
Flooring	○	○	○

THE FEATURES

	✗	✓	♥
Kitchen Cabinets	○	○	○
Kitchen Apppliances	○	○	○
Washer/Dryer	○	○	○
Fireplace	○	○	○
Patio/Balcony	○	○	○
Pool	○	○	○
Landscaping	○	○	○
A/C/Heating	○	○	○
Roof	○	○	○
Windows	○	○	○
Doors	○	○	○
Sprinkler System	○	○	○
Parking	○	○	○
Other	○	○	○

NOTES ABOUT THE NEIGHBORHOOD

Appearance: _____

Traffic: _____

Safety/Security: _____

Schools: _____

HOA: _____

Other: _____

ADDITIONAL NOTES: _____

_____

_____

_____

_____

AGENTS INFORMATION

Agents Name: _____

Agent Phone Number: _____

Open House: _____

OVERALL RATING: ☆ ☆ ☆ ☆ ☆

Property Address: _____

House Nickname: _____

NMLS#: _____ Price: _____

#Bedrooms: _____ #Bathrooms: _____ #Car Garage: _____

House sq/ft: _____ Lot sq/ft: _____ Age of House: _____

THE HOME

	✘	✔	♥
Exterior Condition	○	○	○
Curve Appeal	○	○	○
Floorplan	○	○	○
Kitchen	○	○	○
Family Room	○	○	○
Dining Room	○	○	○
Laundry Room	○	○	○
Master Bedroom	○	○	○
Master Bathroom	○	○	○
Extra Bedrooms	○	○	○
Extra Bathrooms	○	○	○
Closets	○	○	○
Storage Space	○	○	○
Flooring	○	○	○

THE FEATURES

	✘	✔	♥
Kitchen Cabinets	○	○	○
Kitchen Apppliances	○	○	○
Washer/Dryer	○	○	○
Fireplace	○	○	○
Patio/Balcony	○	○	○
Pool	○	○	○
Landscaping	○	○	○
A/C/Heating	○	○	○
Roof	○	○	○
Windows	○	○	○
Doors	○	○	○
Sprinkler System	○	○	○
Parking	○	○	○
Other	○	○	○

NOTES ABOUT THE NEIGHBORHOOD

Appearance: _____

Traffic: _____

Safety/Security: _____

Schools: _____

HOA: _____

Other: _____

ADDITIONAL NOTES: _____

_____

_____

_____

_____

AGENTS INFORMATION

Agents Name: _____

Agent Phone Number: _____

Open House: _____

OVERALL RATING: ☆ ☆ ☆ ☆ ☆

Property Address: _____

House Nickname: _____

NMLS#: _____   Price: _____

#Bedrooms: _____   #Bathrooms: _____   #Car Garage: _____

House sq/ft: _____   Lot sq/ft: _____   Age of House: _____

THE HOME

	✗	✓	♥
Exterior Condition	○	○	○
Curve Appeal	○	○	○
Floorplan	○	○	○
Kitchen	○	○	○
Family Room	○	○	○
Dining Room	○	○	○
Laundry Room	○	○	○
Master Bedroom	○	○	○
Master Bathroom	○	○	○
Extra Bedrooms	○	○	○
Extra Bathrooms	○	○	○
Closets	○	○	○
Storage Space	○	○	○
Flooring	○	○	○

THE FEATURES

	✗	✓	♥
Kitchen Cabinets	○	○	○
Kitchen Apppliances	○	○	○
Washer/Dryer	○	○	○
Fireplace	○	○	○
Patio/Balcony	○	○	○
Pool	○	○	○
Landscaping	○	○	○
A/C/Heating	○	○	○
Roof	○	○	○
Windows	○	○	○
Doors	○	○	○
Sprinkler System	○	○	○
Parking	○	○	○
Other	○	○	○

NOTES ABOUT THE NEIGHBORHOOD

Appearance: _____

Traffic: _____

Safety/Security: _____

Schools: _____

HOA: _____

Other: _____

ADDITIONAL NOTES: _____

_____
_____
_____
_____

AGENTS INFORMATION

Agents Name: _____

Agent Phone Number: _____

Open House: _____

OVERALL RATING: ☆ ☆ ☆ ☆ ☆

| Property Address: _____ |
| House Nickname: _____ |
| NMLS#: _____ Price: _____ |
| #Bedrooms: _____ #Bathrooms: _____ #Car Garage: _____ |
| House sq/ft: _____ Lot sq/ft: _____ Age of House: _____ |

THE HOME

	X	**✓**	**♥**
Exterior Condition	○	○	○
Curve Appeal	○	○	○
Floorplan	○	○	○
Kitchen	○	○	○
Family Room	○	○	○
Dining Room	○	○	○
Laundry Room	○	○	○
Master Bedroom	○	○	○
Master Bathroom	○	○	○
Extra Bedrooms	○	○	○
Extra Bathrooms	○	○	○
Closets	○	○	○
Storage Space	○	○	○
Flooring	○	○	○

THE FEATURES

	X	**✓**	**♥**
Kitchen Cabinets	○	○	○
Kitchen Apppliances	○	○	○
Washer/Dryer	○	○	○
Fireplace	○	○	○
Patio/Balcony	○	○	○
Pool	○	○	○
Landscaping	○	○	○
A/C/Heating	○	○	○
Roof	○	○	○
Windows	○	○	○
Doors	○	○	○
Sprinkler System	○	○	○
Parking	○	○	○
Other	○	○	○

NOTES ABOUT THE NEIGHBORHOOD

Appearance: _____
Traffic: _____
Safety/Security: _____
Schools: _____
HOA: _____
Other: _____

ADDITIONAL NOTES: _____

_____
_____
_____
_____

AGENTS INFORMATION

Agents Name: _____
Agent Phone Number: _____
Open House: _____

OVERALL RATING: ☆ ☆ ☆ ☆ ☆

Property Address: _____

House Nickname: _____

NMLS#: _____ Price: _____

#Bedrooms: _____ #Bathrooms: _____ #Car Garage: _____

House sq/ft: _____ Lot sq/ft: _____ Age of House: _____

THE HOME

	✗	✓	♥
Exterior Condition	○	○	○
Curve Appeal	○	○	○
Floorplan	○	○	○
Kitchen	○	○	○
Family Room	○	○	○
Dining Room	○	○	○
Laundry Room	○	○	○
Master Bedroom	○	○	○
Master Bathroom	○	○	○
Extra Bedrooms	○	○	○
Extra Bathrooms	○	○	○
Closets	○	○	○
Storage Space	○	○	○
Flooring	○	○	○

THE FEATURES

	✗	✓	♥
Kitchen Cabinets	○	○	○
Kitchen Apppliances	○	○	○
Washer/Dryer	○	○	○
Fireplace	○	○	○
Patio/Balcony	○	○	○
Pool	○	○	○
Landscaping	○	○	○
A/C/Heating	○	○	○
Roof	○	○	○
Windows	○	○	○
Doors	○	○	○
Sprinkler System	○	○	○
Parking	○	○	○
Other	○	○	○

NOTES ABOUT THE NEIGHBORHOOD

Appearance: _____

Traffic: _____

Safety/Security: _____

Schools: _____

HOA: _____

Other: _____

ADDITIONAL NOTES: _____

_____

_____

_____

_____

AGENTS INFORMATION

Agents Name: _____

Agent Phone Number: _____

Open House: _____

OVERALL RATING: ☆☆☆☆☆

Property Address: _____
House Nickname: _____
NMLS#: _____ Price: _____
#Bedrooms: _____ #Bathrooms: _____ #Car Garage: _____
House sq/ft: _____ Lot sq/ft: _____ Age of House: _____

THE HOME

	X	✓	♥
Exterior Condition	○	○	○
Curve Appeal	○	○	○
Floorplan	○	○	○
Kitchen	○	○	○
Family Room	○	○	○
Dining Room	○	○	○
Laundry Room	○	○	○
Master Bedroom	○	○	○
Master Bathroom	○	○	○
Extra Bedrooms	○	○	○
Extra Bathrooms	○	○	○
Closets	○	○	○
Storage Space	○	○	○
Flooring	○	○	○

THE FEATURES

	X	✓	♥
Kitchen Cabinets	○	○	○
Kitchen Apppliances	○	○	○
Washer/Dryer	○	○	○
Fireplace	○	○	○
Patio/Balcony	○	○	○
Pool	○	○	○
Landscaping	○	○	○
A/C/Heating	○	○	○
Roof	○	○	○
Windows	○	○	○
Doors	○	○	○
Sprinkler System	○	○	○
Parking	○	○	○
Other	○	○	○

NOTES ABOUT THE NEIGHBORHOOD

Appearance: _____
Traffic: _____
Safety/Security: _____
Schools: _____
HOA: _____
Other: _____

ADDITIONAL NOTES: _____
_____
_____
_____
_____

AGENTS INFORMATION

Agents Name: _____
Agent Phone Number: _____
Open House: _____

OVERALL RATING: ☆ ☆ ☆ ☆ ☆

Property Address: _____
House Nickname: _____
NMLS#: _____   Price: _____
#Bedrooms: _____   #Bathrooms: _____   #Car Garage: _____
House sq/ft: _____   Lot sq/ft: _____   Age of House: _____

THE HOME

	✗	✓	♥
Exterior Condition	○	○	○
Curve Appeal	○	○	○
Floorplan	○	○	○
Kitchen	○	○	○
Family Room	○	○	○
Dining Room	○	○	○
Laundry Room	○	○	○
Master Bedroom	○	○	○
Master Bathroom	○	○	○
Extra Bedrooms	○	○	○
Extra Bathrooms	○	○	○
Closets	○	○	○
Storage Space	○	○	○
Flooring	○	○	○

THE FEATURES

	✗	✓	♥
Kitchen Cabinets	○	○	○
Kitchen Apppliances	○	○	○
Washer/Dryer	○	○	○
Fireplace	○	○	○
Patio/Balcony	○	○	○
Pool	○	○	○
Landscaping	○	○	○
A/C/Heating	○	○	○
Roof	○	○	○
Windows	○	○	○
Doors	○	○	○
Sprinkler System	○	○	○
Parking	○	○	○
Other	○	○	○

NOTES ABOUT THE NEIGHBORHOOD

Appearance: _____
Traffic: _____
Safety/Security: _____
Schools: _____
HOA: _____
Other: _____

ADDITIONAL NOTES: _____
_____
_____
_____
_____

AGENTS INFORMATION

Agents Name: _____
Agent Phone Number: _____
Open House: _____

OVERALL RATING: ☆ ☆ ☆ ☆ ☆

www.ingramcontent.com/pod-product-compliance
Lightning Source LLC
Chambersburg PA
CBHW070316240526
45467CB00045B/420